Critical Guides to French Texts

26 Madame de Lafayette: La Princesse de Clèves

Critical Guides to French Texts

EDITED BY ROGER LITTLE, WOLFGANG VAN EMDEN, DAVID WILLIAMS

MADAME DE LAFAYETTE

La Princesse de Clèves

Second edition

J. W. Scott

Senior Lecturer in French,
University of Southampton

Grant & Cutler Ltd
1997

© Grant & Cutler Ltd 1997

ISBN 0 7293 0400 0

First edition 1983

Second edition 1997

DEPÓSITO LEGAL: V. 2.700 - 1997

Printed in Spain by
Artes Gráficas Soler, S.A., Valencia
for
GRANT & CUTLER LTD
55-57 GREAT MARLBOROUGH STREET, LONDON W1V 2AY

Contents

Prefatory Note

The text on which the first edition (1983) of this study was based, edited by Antoine Adam (No.82 in the GF-Flammarion series), has since been replaced by the edition by Jean Mesnard (No.757 in the same series), first published by the Imprimerie Nationale in 1980. References to the text of *La Princesse de Clèves* are now therefore in the form 'p.68/109', the first reference being to the Adam edition (1966) and the second to that by Mesnard (1996).

Italicized numbers in parentheses, followed by page references, refer to the numbered items in the select bibliography at the end of this volume.

1. Introduction

La Princesse de Clèves first appeared, anonymously, in Paris in March 1678. No doubt the great majority of those readers of fiction who knew of its forthcoming publication expected just another short romance, and indeed – as we shall see – many of the formal and other characteristics of the work are rooted in literary tradition. Nevertheless, the public was in for something of a surprise: historically speaking, *La Princesse de Clèves* 'donne au roman ses lettres de noblesse, dépeint sans complaisance le monde cruel... et renverse les règles du jeu'.[1]

What were these 'rules', and of what 'game'? The allusion is clearly, on one level, to a body of literary conventions regulating the narrative fiction of the time, consecrations in imaginative writing of certain assumptions made about aspects of society and about the nature of the world in general by a representative readership. In other words, there was a public that 'knew what it liked', and that was in the main provided for by run-of-the-mill novelists. What did this public like?

One can hardly dismiss the totality of prose fiction in France before 1678 (or in Europe generally) by defining it as the confirmation of the reader's illusions by the narration of an allegedly 'true' story (although the definition could still be applied with some justification to a good deal of fiction of our own day), but it is undeniably the case that great tracts of the 'pays de la Romancie'[2] at that time are nourished by wishful thinking. The 'novels' of the period are indeed *romances*: usually very long and in numerous

---

[1] Michel Mercier, *Le Roman féminin*, P.U.F., 1976, p.230.

[2] The expression is borrowed from the Jesuit Father Bougeant, active as a literary critic in the early eighteenth century

volumes, they tend to deal with the protracted adventures of a young marriageable couple, repeatedly separated before final reunion – the man often temporarily removed by his responsibilities as a soldier or courtier, the girl by disasters such as shipwreck or abduction by pirates.[3] It is easy to laugh at such a pattern as a model for the shape of significant human existence. But one's laughter is modified, at least, by the reflection that in the seventeenth century absences on military or diplomatic business could be prolonged and that travel could be arduous and subject to hazard: there *were* shipwrecks and pirates in reality. And – together with varied deeds of daring – they provided elements of glamour, excitement and vicarious danger for a reading public whose membership, no longer confined to the nobility, was becoming increasingly sedentary and middle-class, whether its activities were mercantile, financial, legal, administrative, or simply domestic. As Madame de Sévigné wrote, with exemplary self-awareness, of her own response to the work of one of these contemporary popular novelists (La Calprenède): 'la violence des passions, la grandeur des événements..., tout cela m'entraîne comme une petite fille' (letter to her daughter, Mme de Grignan, 12 July 1671). In our own times the phenomena of shipwrecks and pirates, or their equivalents, still have a role to play – although displaced further down the socio-cultural scale – in the strip-cartoon. The novels of the first half of the seventeenth century in France are not so much transcriptions of observable day-to-day crude social reality, as *normative* manifestations, representations of what it might be desirable for men or women to do or say. As Madame de Sévigné puts it (still of the work of La Calprenède): 'pour les sentiments..., ils sont d'une perfection qui remplit mon idée sur les belles âmes' (letter to Mme de Grignan, 15 July 1671).

A wish is often father to a thought, and there are quite a number of 'thoughts', in this sense, lurking in the pages of the works I am referring to. One of these thoughts is really a wishful *belief*

---

[3] For more detail, and supporting material, see *1* and *2* in the Select Bibliography.

concerning the relation of the sexes, implicit in the fact that, as has already been suggested, the typical romance ends with the marriage of the protagonists: a woman, when asked by the 'right' man, says 'Yes', and lives happily ever after. This is a very important, and enduring, belief about men and women, but it is a belief that does not always seem to be supported by the evidence, nor is it accepted uncritically at all periods of history by *all* thinkers or writers. It is accepted, with important provisos, by a novelist like Jane Austen. It *is not* accepted, apparently, by the author of *La Princesse de Clèves*: the work *begins* (virtually) with marriage, ends with refusal and isolation, and can even be interpreted as implying that the 'right' man does not exist. This is another sense, perhaps, in which the work may be said to 'reject the rules of the game'.

What has just been said above about seventeenth-century French romances is, however, a generalization: the fiction of the time is by no means so monolithic as I may have seemed to suggest, nor were the upper reaches of the society in which it appeared noticeably more male-dominated than our own. If women said 'Yes', on this cultural level, it was in the main because they *wished* to say 'Yes'. What is at issue here is not social enslavement but a metaphysic – a view of reality in which the complementariness of the sexes was thought to be most fittingly expressed by the concept of marriage. The romance, whether heroic or pastoral in emphasis – that is to say whether the setting and pattern of events are concerned predominantly with valiant prowess or with gentler models of existence among shepherds and their shepherdesses in a conventional Arcady – is not always simply concerned with successful male pursuit, but often also presents women attempting, through self-analysis and self-questioning, to understand themselves and to clarify their desires and values (the author of two of the most popular romances of the century – *Artamène ou le Grand Cyrus*, 1649, and *Clélie*, 1654 – was a woman, Madeleine de Scudéry[4]). Then there are exceptions here and there to the general rule of the assumption of the wedded state as a safely desirable terminal situation; there are tales in

---

[4] Bibliography, 3.

which the final emotional condition of the female protagonist – married or not – is unhappy (although these stories – many of those, for example, of Madame de Villedieu[5] – tend to deal, unlike *La Princesse de Clèves*, more or less moralistically with women who are presented as in some way *deserving* their unhappiness); and we must not overlook the important existence as a combining element in seventeenth-century French fiction of the tradition of the *nouvelle*.

The *nouvelle* is the descendant, in French language and culture, of the Italian *novella*, a literary form most familiar, perhaps, through the fourteenth-century examples of it that compose Boccaccio's *Decameron*. The *nouvelle*, like the romance, is a narrative fiction (usually in prose), but of much more modest proportions, more decided in tragic (or comic) tone, and constructed – rather like a short story with more space devoted to presentation of character – on a pattern of tightly-related events that often culminate in a dramatic climax of surprise. By the time *La Princesse de Clèves* appeared in 1678 the *nouvelle* was a well-established French genre, and it is clear that the work we are interested in is as closely related to *this* form as it is to that of the romance. Indeed, the author of *La Princesse de Clèves* had herself already produced, it seems, one work of fiction in each genre: in 1669/70, *Zayde*, which, although considerably shorter than the average run of the type, is assimilable to the novel/romance, and already in 1662, *La Princesse de Montpensier* (*5a*) which is undeniably a *nouvelle*.

La Princesse de Clèves contains little, then, in a *formal* sense that can be claimed as a totally new departure. What is it then about this text that (to quote Michel Mercier again) conferred 'ses lettres de noblesse' upon the art of prose fiction? It seems to the present writer that *La Princesse de Clèves* is of outstanding value because of:

(1) the accuracy of its notations in the field of psychology and the emotions (to put it another way, the quality, verifiable from our own experience, of its author's perceptions: we are dealing here with a writer of considerable acuity of mind).

(2) the way in which these notations or perceptions are expressed –

---

[5] Bibliography, *4* and *5*.

i.e., its style: the writing is characterised by a tone that is at once familiar and – while avoiding moralising – sustainedly serious and objective.

(3) the nature of the protagonist: like, it could be said, the central character of Racine's *Phèdre*, she decides her own destiny in a situation that she has not chosen. It would be difficult to argue that she 'deserves her unhappiness'.

(4) what can be referred to, broadly speaking, as the *philosophical* implications of the work, which present us with more than a hint that the desiderata of the two sexes are different in some respects, and may indeed be irreconcilable: the tale ends 'badly' even though the princess and Nemours are, we are told, well suited 'naturally'. And on this the author offers no guiding comment; the reader is left to his own meditations on a text that is *problematic*.

(5) (last by no means least) its *structure*. It is this aspect of the work that I propose to examine first.

2. Structure

In general terms, the word 'structure' refers to the manner of building or organizing material into a satisfactory whole. Since, in the context of literature, this involves consideration of the arranging of the component parts of a work, some critics prefer to think of it as an aspect of *style*. It is easier, perhaps, to identify it and to perceive its operation if it is dealt with separately. In whatever category one places it, however, structure is undeniably an indispensable element in the successful control by an artist of raw experience so that it may be presented meaningfully. There is no such thing as an unstructured work of art: even such apparently formless and inclusive works as the 'stream of consciousness' novels of James Joyce or the prose fictions of Samuel Beckett operate through selection and emphasis, and analysis of a text can help us, by elucidating the proportions and other relations of its constituent parts, to appreciate how it 'works' as a cultural artefact.

Virginia Woolf[6] once claimed that *La Princesse de Clèves* is compounded of such intensity of vision and accuracy of expression that its form is as it were invisible. But form it has, none the less. On one level of reality, it is concerned with events in European history, intrigues at the court of France, and the emotional and moral maturing of a sixteen-year-old girl of noble family, during a period of some months of 1558 and 1559. These questions are presented to us in about one hundred and fifty pages. The theoretically enormous mass of data available has been sifted, consciously or unconsciously, by the author's preoccupations. What has been rejected, what has been retained, what has been underlined? How has the matter been

---

[6] *The Moment*, 'On re-reading novels' (*Collected Essays*, II, Hogarth Press, 1966, p.126).

shaped by the pressures of the themes so as to carry adequately what is judged to be essential?

Clearly, a great deal of total, global 'reality' has been omitted or condensed. Protestantism, for example, which was of cardinal importance in determining the pattern of political events of the period, is reduced to not much more than a passing reference (pp.90-91/134-35), while – to turn our attention from the spiritual register to the material – no gastronomic details whatsoever are given of the various celebratory entertainments mentioned as being offered by royalty or nobility. On the other hand, a considerable proportion of the first fifty-five pages of the text is given over to evocation in various ways of the tensions and preoccupations at court *arising out of* aspects of the political history of the time: 'L'ambition et la galanterie', we are told, 'étaient l'âme de cette cour, et occupaient également les hommes et les femmes... une sorte d'agitation sans désordre...la rendait très agréable, mais aussi très dangereuse pour une jeune personne' (pp.44-45/80-81). The function of court life in the environmental conditioning of the heroine having been thus established, the proportion of the text devoted to happenings not strictly relevant to her development then begins to decrease, once she has grasped (and the reader also) that (as her mother tells her) 'si vous jugez sur les apparences en ce lieu-ci, vous serez souvent trompée' (p.56/94). The author treats Mme de Chartres herself in much the same way – i.e., functionally. The education of the princess until beyond her fifteenth birthday is entirely in the hands of her mother (p.41/76), but since the tale is concerned with what the young woman will ultimately become – with how she as a free individual will *use* her education (or fail to transcend it), we need to see her in a critical situation deprived of the possibility of resort to her usual counsellor. So the author removes the mother, by illness, one fifth of the way through the book (p.68/109), leaving the daughter to face alone her husband and the situation brought into being by her attraction towards Nemours. A similar functional process operates in the timing of the appearance in the narrative of Nemours and Clèves, and in the relative emphasis initially given them. Both men are introduced in the same paragraph (p.37/71-72), and noticeably, although not excessively, before the first mention of Mlle de Chartres herself (p.40/76), but whereas Clèves is simply described as being 'brave et magnifique' (that is, with a taste for well-conducted social ostentation), and as possessing 'une prudence qui ne se trouve guère avec la jeunesse', we are told much more about Nemours, so that when the young woman meets him for the first time (p.53/91), her marriage to Clèves having taken place during the (again, functional) absence of Nemours in Bruxelles, the reader knows, while she does not, that 'peu de celles à qui il s'était attaché, se pouvaient vanter de lui avoir résisté', that 'il avait plusieurs maîtresses, mais il était difficile de deviner celle qu'il aimait véritablement', and that his relations with 'la Reine Dauphine' are so cordial that they 'avait souvent donné lieu de croire qu'il levait les yeux jusqu'à elle' (p.38/72). The reader thus becomes, as in tragedy (and some kinds of comedy), a privileged spectator, in possession of information denied provisionally to a protagonist, and consequently invited to suffer in anticipation with a representative human figure from whom he is none the less detached by the basic conditions of the aesthetic experience. Thus primed, the reader or spectator can simultaneously judge and sympathize.

Enough will have been said already to make it clear that in *La Princesse de Clèves* we have to do with a text that concentrates attention on certain focal aspects of essential human experience by exploiting selectively the possibilities of life in a strictly delimited social area, that of the court. The court itself functions in the work as a symbol of the arena of existence set for the operation of decision and destiny: it is at one and the same time a small world, set apart so that we can see its frontiers, and representative of the world of human affairs in general. The princess can absent herself from the round of activities at court only very briefly without questions being asked. The privacy of her own room in Paris, the rural quiet of the estate at Coulommiers, are fragile and temporary retreats from which return to the hazards of observed conflict is obligatory as one of the rules of the game, and it is worth noting that once she has rejected Nemours and retired from court, 'sa vie', we are told, 'fut assez courte' (p.180/239). However temporarily, Coulommiers functions as a place of liberation: it is at Coulommiers that Mme de Clèves finds it possible to tell her husband as much of the truth as is compatible with dignity and self-respect; it is at Coulommiers, set in the forest, that Nemours sees her in what is effectively a state of nature, unreservedly true to one normally suppressed element of her personality (p.155/208-09).

Once we have accepted that the author of *La Princesse de Clèves* is interested predominantly in isolating and communicating the movements of the emotions and the moral sense, it is easier to grasp the notion that events are being chosen and used for a purpose. Indeed, a member of the work's first public, the young mathematician Fontenelle, made it clear that, although he disapproved of the hidden presence of Nemours at the heroine's confession to her husband because it was too reminiscent of the sort of adventure to be found in the long heroic novel, he understood the *function* of the episode. 'Je suis ravi que Monsieur de Nemours sache la conversation', he wrote, 'mais [pretending to be a moral censor] je suis au désespoir qu'il écoute' (*Le Mercure galant*, May 1678). Until this point in the narrative, Nemours has been inhibited in his actions by uncertainty about the heroine's feelings (p.124/173). For the story to continue to develop, this uncertainty needs to be removed, and his presence at the interview does precisely this. (That I am not misinterpreting Fontenelle's words seems to be confirmed by his generalized enthusiasm, expressed elsewhere in his review, for what he refers to as 'le *plan* de l'auteur'.)

From this point of view, many of the happenings and situations in the book can be seen as *devices* – although very 'real-seeming', *vraisemblable* devices. I have already mentioned the functional necessity of the death of Mme de Chartres. Equally necessary is the death of Clèves, which confronts the princess with an emotionally more complex situation than any she has yet found herself in, and provides her with the need to understand herself more fully and to try to establish a moral code more adequate to the world as she now sees it. In the texture of the work as a whole this device is itself a product of the emotional state of Clèves, generated in its turn by his passionately uncritical response to the scrupulously limited report of the 'gentilhomme' on his 'shadowing' of Nemours, this mission in its turn being a product of the sexual jealousy of Clèves himself.

This particular group of sequent movements of feeling and action is only one of many examples which could be adduced to indicate the organic nature of so many of these events, related to each other and to the work as a whole as parts of what could be seen as a deterministic pattern of cause and effect. An interest in psychological causality is of course a characteristic of many writers in the seventeenth century. We are most familiar with its manifestations, perhaps, in the French theatre of the time: a structural examination of, let us say, Racine's *Phèdre* (which was first performed in 1677, the year before the publication of *La Princesse de Clèves*), reveals that it is built on a series of alternating events and reactions to events (for example, the rumour of Thésée's death and all that follows) that leads the queen down a spiral course to her confession and suicide. In the same way, *La Princesse de Clèves* could be analysed into sections that in their function – and indeed in their number – are similar to the divisions of one possible scheme for the five-act play (the arrangement of the work as we have it in four 'tomes' is the result of compromise between the needs of the text on the one hand, and on the other, the constraints of seventeenth-century printing technology and the convenience of the publisher):

Act I   Exposition: introduction to the glamour and danger of court life, and to two of the protagonists (Clèves and Nemours). Presentation of Mlle de Chartres and meeting with Clèves (pp.35-44/69-79).

Act II   Rivalry of Clèves and Guise, decided in favour of the former for political reasons (political intrigues and history continue intermittently to provide a backcloth for the action until p.90/133). Marriage of Mlle de Chartres and Clèves and first meeting with Nemours, episode of the maréchal de Saint-André's ball, suspicion of a link between Nemours and 'la reine dauphine', death of Mme de Chartres (pp.45-68/80-109).

Act III   Approach to the first crisis: episode of Mme de Tournon, illustrating further for the princess the inscrutability of aspects of behaviour. Nemours's visit of condolence. Husband's first illness (preparing us for the second). The king's views on astrology (which sensitize the reader to the question of individual destiny). Nemours steals the portrait. Preparations for the tournament. Nemours's accident, revealing to the princess – and to Guise – the extent of her involvement (an incident re-used in a modified way, two hundred years later, by another great novelist, Leo Tolstoy, in his *Anna Karenina*). The incident of the lost letter which motivates the heroine's awareness of her emotional and moral condition through hatred of Nemours and subsequent 'reconciliation'. Flight to Coulommiers and the confession (pp.69-125/110-74).

Act IV Jealous agony of Clèves. Preparations for the marriage of the king's daughter, death of the king and fulfilment of the astrologer's prediction. 'La Cour changea entièrement de face' (p.147/199). Second flight to Coulommiers, pursued by Nemours. Death of Clèves (pp.126-64/175-219).

Act V Second crisis, catastrophe, and epilogue: continued pursuit by Nemours (the rented room and the 'jardin hors des faubourgs') culminating in the meeting arranged by the widow's uncle. Rejection of Nemours. Pursuit to the Pyrenees (no doubt a spatial symbol of the extent within societal limits of the lover's ardour) and ultimate renunciation (pp.165-80/220-39).

The structure of *La Princesse de Clèves* is assimilable, then, to that of a drama. In addition, the emotional and moral conflicts with which the work is concerned are frequently communicated to the reader by means of *techniques* which are also associated with the serious classical theatre: confrontations, for example (the princess and her mother, the princess and her husband, the princess and Nemours), or monologues, in which a protagonist evaluates past action or engages in heart-searching which will lead, perhaps, to decision, whether or not it is followed by future action. A representative instance of this is the isolation of the princess so that she may examine herself, once the substitute letter has been fabricated: 'Madame de Clèves demeura seule, et sitôt qu'elle ne fut plus soutenue par cette joie que donne la présence de ce que l'on aime, elle revint comme d'un songe...' (p.118/166). The monologue is also used as a way of ensuring that the reader is fully aware of the authenticity or otherwise of a character's utterances. If characters make statements when confronting each other, they may be lying, but when Nemours, for example, whose consciousness is not often revealed to us, is given a *monologue* at a crucial moment in the story (p.168/224-25), when the princess is apparently weakening in her attitude, we can see that the man she thinks she loves still possesses unimpaired his predatory faculties. And it is no doubt of some significance that readers discussing *La Princesse de Clèves* often refer casually and without reflexion to the two 'big *scenes*' of the confession and the renunciation.

I am not suggesting, however, that this *nouvelle* is really a play which its author mistakenly decided to compose as a piece of narrative prose. It is quite normal for a narrative writer to use dramatic methods, for example the presentation of characters as speaking and acting. Indeed, the earliest piece of literary comment known to us – the *Poetics* of Aristotle, which dates from the fourth century B.C.– praises Homer for 'speaking as little as possible in his own person', and for introducing, after a few preparatory lines, characters who speak in *their* own persons (*Poetics*, III.3). The author of *La Princesse de Clèves*, too, uses dramatic methods in this way, as an aid to the narrative, and as a means to an end, namely the identification of motive. (Not all admirers of *La Princesse de Clèves* have understood this – there have been various attempts to *dramatize* it, none of them successful. The two best-known are perhaps the worst: the earlier in date is a play, conceived as a vehicle for the actress Sarah Bernhardt by the critic Jules Lemaitre[7], while the more recent piece is a film, made in 1961 with a scenario by Jean Cocteau, in which the quality of the photographic composition fails to compensate for disastrous tampering with the substance of the *nouvelle*: 'dramatic moments', in which actors are actually *seen*

---

[7] To be found in vol. III of his *Théâtre* (Calmann-Lévy, 1908).

listening behind partitions, and pretty pictures, whether of castles on the River Loire or of the face of a pensive heroine in close-up, are no substitute for the real concerns and *modus operandi* of our text, namely, clarification of the processes of thought and feeling *through language*.)

One other important structural device needs to be mentioned. There is self-evidently nothing in the title of *La Princesse de Clèves*, nor – until very near the end – is there any specific statement in the text, that excludes the possibility of a happy outcome. And yet the reader does very soon find himself excluding precisely this possibility. Why? What is it in the texture of the work that leads us, as we read, to expect disaster? Partly, of course, the *tone*. But equally, the fact that, broadly speaking, all the important developments of the narrative in this direction are *prepared*: there are early warning indications. And of these, the most interesting are those communicated to the reader through the use of what I shall call proleptic (i.e. 'anticipatory') *analogues*.

An analogue is a phenomenon that, in any given context, manifests similarities of structure and function with a phenomenon in another context (without necessarily being identical in all respects). In comparative anatomy, for example, the wings of birds are thought of as *analogues* of (analogous to) the front legs of quadrupeds. In human life, analogues may be found in such things as omens, portents, dreams, intuitions, obsessive images: when the mother of Louis XIV, Anne of Austria, was dying of cancer in 1665, she recalled the death from the same malady, nearly twenty years before, of a nun whom she had visited in the Val-de-Grâce convent in Paris, and the memory of whose agony and courage had never left her (see Bibliography, *6*, I, p.333; IV, p.365). Coincidence, one might say – many people die of cancer. But the queen mother herself thought of the death of the nun as a premonitory act of God's Providence. As a phenomenon of human consciousness, it was an analogue. And in *literature*, when the course of a life – real or fictional – comes to be written down, such analogues, skilfully handled, can be used to sharpen the reader's sense of destiny. An obvious example from *La Princesse de Clèves* is the configuration and organic function in the text of the episode concerning Mme de Tournon. This 'digression' (as some critics still call it) is essentially the story of a widow publicly believed to be a paragon of virtue and revealed after her death to have maintained an intimate relationship with two men simultaneously. It is presented to the reader significantly early in the work (pp.69-80/110-22). Equally significantly, the revelation is made to Mme de Clèves herself, at a time when she is vulnerable emotionally (her mother, on whom she has been morally dependent, having just died), and it shocks her, not only because she still finds it difficult not to accept appearances in general as reliable guides to truth but also because Mme de Tournon in particular was, as she says, 'une des personnes du monde qui me plaisait davantage et qui paraissait avoir autant de sagesse que de mérite' (p.69/110). Significantly also, the news of Mme de Tournon's duplicity is imparted to the princess by Clèves, with the accompanying comment: 'je me trouve si heureux de vous avoir que je ne saurais assez admirer mon bonheur' (p.69/110). In addition, he repeats to his wife the statement he made to one of Mme de Tournon's lovers, his friend Sancerre, namely: 'la sincérité me touche d'une telle sorte que je crois que si ma maîtresse, et même ma femme, m'avouait que quelqu'un lui plût, j'en serais affligé sans en être aigri. Je quitterais le personnage d'amant ou de mari pour la conseiller et pour la plaindre' (p.76/116-17). Furthermore, this episode contains a reference to the apparently insignificant and subordinate incident of the quarrel and reconciliation of Henri II and Mme de Valentinois, that hinges on the disappearance of a ring given as a love-token (pp.73-74/113-14), and which in effect prefigures the later theft by Nemours of the portrait of Mme de Clèves.

The relevance of this episode to the pattern of subsequent events involving the protagonists of the main narrative is clear. In the tale of Mme de Tournon the princess is presented, not only with an example of the unreliability of social appearances, an example that plays a part in her experiential apprenticeship, but also with a foreshadowing of one possible direction that her own moral evolution might follow. That there is authorial intention here is indeed more than half explicit, since the text immediately following her husband's statement about sincerity, quoted above, tells us that 'ces paroles firent rougir Madame de Clèves, et elle y trouva un certain rapport avec l'état où elle était, qui la surprit et qui lui donna un trouble dont elle fut longtemps à se remettre'. This reaction to a compliment on her supposed freedom from the frailties of other women, shortly after her dying mother has told her that 'si quelque chose était capable de troubler le bonheur que j'espère en sortant de ce monde, ce serait de vous voir tomber comme les autres femmes' (p.68/108), not only sensitizes the princess herself (bearing in mind that she only exists as part of the world created by the author) to the potential dangers of her situation, but is also a signal to the imagination of the reader that stimulates him to forecast possibilities involving Clèves as well, since it is he who pays the compliment. When one of these possibilities comes to pass – the failure of the husband's stated theoretical principle when tested against reality in the confession scene – the reader's memory ironically recalls the past. And the *range* of future developments is conditioned, if not determined, by the kind of information that emerges from this 'digression' concerning Mme de Tournon: precisely because of the nature and emphasis of elements of the case, it is difficult for the intelligent and sensitive reader to entertain any other ultimate options for the princess, exposed as she is to the standards of the society into which she has been brought, and motivated by the high ambitions that she has learnt from her mother (for example, 'aimer son mari, et en être aimée'), than retreat or shameful surrender, exile or defeat.

This particular proleptic analogue, like the main plot, is fictitious. The *names* of the actors in the episode – those of Sancerre, Estouteville, Mme de Tournon herself – are to be found in chronicles, certainly, but there is no record of the events in which they play their part having taken place in historical reality. The same is true, as one might expect, of some more limited actions that function proleptically; for example, the entry of Nemours into the ballroom, which he effects, we are told, by climbing 'par-dessus quelque siège' (p.53/91) – a discreet, apparently trivial preparation, in an eminently social register, for the vigorous personal initiative he later manifests in escalading the fence at Coulommiers. But the

majority of the remaining analogues of any importance are
constituted by patterns of events taken from historical sources, and
indeed, the exploitation of history in general is so central to the way
in which our text 'works' that it merits a chapter to itself.

3. The Use of History

There is no shortage in the seventeenth century in France of writers of fiction, as well as composers of chronicles, whose work contains lengthy descriptions of past court festivities, entertainments, balls, ceremonial rituals, characterized by what some economic historians refer to as 'conspicuous consumption'. These descriptions do not, however, operate as 'analogues' in the works which contain them. Their aim is in the main limited and obvious: they are glamorous 'set pieces', designed to suscitate in the reader such emotions as wholehearted admiration of a political order, or of a privileged way of life, or of the persons leading it. But in the case of a highly sophisticated imaginative work like *La Princesse de Clèves*, the function of such commonplace elements is more complicated. It has already been suggested that in our text the court in general has the role of representing symbolically the conditions within which the passions flourish and which at the same time constrain them. In addition, and more precisely, certain historical events are significantly cited so as to suggest to the reader that the protagonists of the *nouvelle* live in a world the majority of whose practised inhabitants accept that marriage is not a question of love but of dynastic alliances or personal advancement, and who accept also that emotionally satisfying sexual relationships are usually formed outside marriage, and unofficially, and may be dangerous. This is well illustrated by, on the one hand, the response of Nemours to the interest shown in him by Elizabeth of England (p.40/75) and, on the other, by the self-inflicted predicament of the vidame de Chartres, terrified for his life in case the letter he has lost should fall into the hands of the queen (p.110/156-57), or the laconic and apparently casual notation (p.36/70) that 'Madame Elisabeth de France, qui fut depuis Reine d'Espagne, commençait à faire paraître... cette incomparable beauté qui lui a été si funeste' – a clear allusion to her

death at the age of twenty-three as the wife of the sombre,
disagreeable Philip II (who, legend had it, caused her to be poisoned,
having discovered a passionate relationship between her and his son
by an earlier marriage, Don Carlos). The betrothal of Elisabeth de
France is also exploited characteristically. A certain amount of the
text which presents this (ceremonial detail, for instance) was clearly
taken by the author, with little alteration, from readily available
chronicles like Pierre Mathieu's *Histoire de France*.[8] But instead of
being used in La Princesse de Clèves in one set piece, it is dispersed
through a considerable area of the work (pp.83/125; 87/131; 93-
95/138-39; 130/180-81; 140-44/192-97) in such a way as to 'point
up' some of the general issues basic to the main fictional plot (partly
through the participation in the betrothal of Mme de Clèves herself).
Interwoven as they are with the lives of Clèves, his wife, and
Nemours, the events of the celebrations take on a disturbing
significance. The contrast between the dignified pageantry
surrounding the betrothal of Elisabeth and the undignified mortal
wounding of her father at the tournament orientates the reader's
attention towards the uncertainty of destiny (this is underlined,
indeed, by the fulfilling of the astrologer's prediction, dismissively
made light of by the king himself): the life of Mme de Clèves has
already been affected by one death – that of her mother – and will be
affected still more by that – equally unexpected by her – of her
husband. And the clear indication that Elisabeth is being used as a
political pawn in the game of international dynastic politics of the
time, in which marriage functioned as a welding of alliances, reminds
us of the harsh limitations of a woman's freedom of choice.

The betrothal of Elisabeth de France can none the less hardly
be claimed as an 'analogue'– it is rather a question of aspects of a
historical event being selectively used for their symbolic possibilities.

---

[8] 1631. The question of the indebtedness of our author to historical sources
of the Valois period has been exhaustively studied in Bibliography, 7. The
transcriptions and adaptations of writings by historiographers that form part
of *La Princesse de Clèves* often manifest one of the characteristic stigmata
of the *nouvelle historique*, viz. psychological 'explanations' of an event that
are absent from the original.

The analogical function in the text of some other historical figures –
in particular Mme de Valentinois and Anne de Boulen (Anne
Boleyn) – is more clear-cut. Both these women are presented in such
a way as to exemplify for Mme de Clèves – 'qui était dans cet âge où
l'on ne croit pas qu'une femme puisse être aimée quand elle a passé
vingt-cinq ans' (p.55/93) – the ambivalence of relationships
(compounded by definition, in the world of the text, of strength and
instability) that are built on sexuality, and the narratives concerning
them thus offer her 'experience' (albeit second-hand) relevant to her
own future. The story of Mme de Valentinois (pp.48/84-85;
55-60/93-99; 141-44/194-97), in addition to its general importance
as an illustration of the warning given by Mme de Chartres not to
trust appearances (p.56/94), provides an example of a woman
retaining control of her lover only at the cost of jealousy and
compromise, prefigures the courtly *demi-monde* to which the
princess would perhaps perforce belong were she to take a lover, and
suggests, through the notation of François Ier distributing his
attentions among a group of mistresses, the potential character of
Nemours. No doubt, against what is said of the promiscuity of one
king is set the fidelity of another, his son (Henri II), who is described
as being loyal to Mme de Valentinois for more than twenty years, but
this is more than balanced by the effect of her definitive relegation to
the shadows on the demise of her royal master. The story of Anne de
Boulen (pp.89-91/133-35), on the other hand, which similarly
presents the vicissitudes of a life based on sexuality, is a much more
cautionary tale. If her ascension to power is as rapid as that of Mme
de Valentinois, her possession of it is of much shorter duration and is
terminated not only abruptly, but by the headsman's axe, and
recollection of these narratives, the reader imagines, operates
unequivocally in the consciousness of the princess as one of the
factors tending to frighten her away from 'le bord du précipice' on
which her mother's death leaves her (p.68/108); certainly the reader
seeking an explanation for the rhetorical question put to Nemours in
the final interview – 'Mais les hommes conservent-ils de la passion
dans ces engagement éternels?' (p.173/231) – may well choose to
think that the author intended it as an indication that Mme de Clèves,

like the reader, still remembers not only Anne's death, but also –
memory sharpened by the bizzarre detail of the apparently
inconsequential ending of the tale ('Henri VIII mourut, étant devenu
d'une grosseur prodigieuse') – the conduct of Anne's husband. In
addition, the attentive reader will notice that the account of Anne's
lamentable career contains, in the 'courses de bague que faisait le
Vicomte de Rochefort' (p.91/135), a preparation for the horse-
exercise scene in which Mme de Clèves allows Nemours to see that
his accident has emotionally disturbed her.

Part of the story of Mme de Valentinois and the whole of that
of Anne de Boulen are communicated to the heroine by, significantly,
'la Reine Dauphine', Mme la Dauphine (her usual alternative style in
the text), better known to most English readers of *La Princesse de
Clèves* as Mary Stuart. In addition, it is she who relates, as part of the
story of Mme de Valentinois, the unhappy tale of her own mother,
Mary of Guise, widow of the Duc de Longueville, and sought in
marriage by three kings. 'Son malheur', says her daughter, 'l'a
donnée au moindre [James V of Scotland] et l'a mise dans un
royaume où elle ne trouve que des peines. On dit que je lui
ressemble; je crains de lui ressembler aussi par sa malheureuse
destinée; et, quelque bonheur qui semble se préparer pour moi, je ne
saurais croire que j'en jouisse', in reply to which, we are told, the as
yet inexperienced Mlle de Chartres 'dit à la reine que ces tristes
pressentiments étaient si mal fondés qu'elle ne les conserverait pas
longtemps, et qu'elle ne devait point douter que son bonheur ne
répondît aux apparences' (pp.48-49/85). Only the least alert of
contemporary readers would have failed to respond to the emotional
and symbolic resonance of this proleptic analogue: the interlinked
disasters of Mary Stuart's history had become a legend in Europe
even before her execution at Fotheringay in 1587, and few educated
French people in the seventeenth century had not heard something of
this unfortunate and attractive queen of Scotland (and briefly queen
of France also), not the least-known aspect of whose appalling
calvary was the series of infatuations that seem to have brought her
little but unhappiness. And the considerable dramatic irony of our
author's use of the figure of 'la Reine Dauphine' is compounded by

the cheerful innocence of Mlle de Chartres, ignorant of her own destiny, attempting to dispel her royal friend's gloomy view of the future.

The use of historical material by writers of fiction was as much a commonplace in seventeenth-century France as it is now in the world of the novel in general. It is broadly true to say that, with the exception of some professional historians, for whom, understandably enough, the *nouvelle historique* was a misleading masquerade, and a few thinkers like Pierre Bayle[9] (who objected to the omission from specifically, *La Princesse de Clèves*, of certain historically accredited crudities of behaviour on the part of Nemours), no objectors have left a record of having raised their voices. This still leaves us, however, with the questions of what the practitioners of the *nouvelle historique* thought they were up to, and what their majority public thought it was reading. As far as the former are concerned, intentions (as is usually the case where a convention is involved) are not often stated. But such admissions as one finds, however vaguely expressed, can be very revealing. For example, the foreword to a work of the kind we are considering by a contemporary of Mme de Lafayette whom we have already mentioned, Mme de Villedieu[10], tells the reader that 'l'on n'y a inséré des noms connus que pour flatter plus agréablement votre imagination', while a similar statement prefacing *La Princesse de Montpensier*, the *nouvelle historique* that is usually taken to be the first essay in fiction by the author of *La Princesse de Clèves*, admits that 'cette histoire... n'a été tirée d'aucun manuscrit qui nous soit demeuré du temps des personnes dont elle parle' and claims that 'l'auteur a jugé plus à propos de prendre des noms connus dans nos histoires [i.e. history books] que de se servir de ceux qu'on trouve dans les romans'.[11] While the last sentence no doubt refers to a

---

[9] *Nouvelles lettres de l'auteur de la Critique générale de l'Histoire du Calvinisme de M. Maimbourg*, Villefranche, 1685. pp.656-58.

[10] *Le Journal amoureux*, 1680, 'Avis au Lecteur'. (First edition, 1669; and see Bibliography 4 and 5.)

[11] *La Princesse de Montpensier*, 1662, 'Avis du Libraire'. The 'Libraire' was Thomas Joly, the Paris printer and bookseller who first published the anonymous work; it is often impossible to know whether, in such cases, the

conscious break with the romance tradition of using figures that were
either mythological or, if historical, drawn, like Alexander the Great,
for example, from very remote epochs, the confession preceding it is
clearly a blunt reminder to the reader that he is none the less about to
confront a fiction. It is a reasonable supposition that the general
public was a willing party to this 'deception' that little attempt was
made to conceal: the imagination can be the more readily liberated
by contact with a past 'Golden Age of gallantry' – very often, in the
nouvelle historique, that of the later Valois kings, which seems to
have had a comparable function in seventeenth-century France to that
operated nowadays for some English readers of fiction by the periods
of the Regency and of the early years of the reign of Victoria (the
strictly historical events that figure in *La Princesse de Clèves* had
taken place roughly a hundred and twenty years before the
publication of the work). And the writers of fiction themselves can
hardly have been unaware of the powerful inducement offered to the
reader to suspend initial disbelief, by the insertion of an imagined
pattern of intrigue with imagined actors into a known scheme of
recorded reality, particularly if, as in *La Princesse de Clèves*, it is
ultimately not so much the 'Golden Age of gallantry' aspect of the
Valois world that may be emphasized, as that chronological segment
of the period that led up to the Wars of Religion, so that the disorder
of the passions manifested at court is paralleled by the turbulence of
the body politic.

As it happens, it is possible to detect our author actually
fostering the device. A few weeks after *La Princesse de Clèves*
appeared (anonymously), Mme de Lafayette committed herself,
tongue in cheek, to making a few remarks on the work, prompted by
a request from one of her correspondents (Lescheraine, secretary to
the Duchesse de Savoie), who – no doubt in an attempt to draw her
on the question of authorship – had asked for her critical opinion. In
her reply (13 April 1678) she wrote (my italics): 'surtout ce que j'y
trouve, c'est une parfaite imitation du monde de la cour et de la

composer of the 'Avis' is genuinely expressing his own opinions, or those of
the author of the text he is publishing.

manière dont on y vit; ... *aussi n'est-ce pas un roman, c'est proprement des mémoires* et c'était, à ce que l'on m'a dit, le titre du livre, mais on l'a changé'. It must be admitted that the opening pages of the *nouvelle* have the tone of memoirs, presenting considerable similarity with, for example, the beginning of chapter five of the *Mémoires* of Mme de Lafayette's friend Mme de Motteville (1621-89; cf. *6*, 1, pp.99-100), in which, the reader is told,

> nous allons voir... de quelle nature est le climat de ce pays qu'on appelle la cour... L'air n'y est jamais doux ni serein pour personne. Ceux mêmes qui, dans l'apparence d'un bonheur tout entier, y sont adorés comme des dieux, sont ceux qui sont les plus menacés de l'orage... ceux mêmes que leurs compatriotes regardent avec envie ne connaissent point de calme... Ils sont toujours malades de cette contagieuse maladie de l'ambition, qui leur ôte le repos, leur ronge le cœur et leur envoie des vapeurs à la tête, qui souvent leur ôte la raison.

Mme de Motteville's text, certainly, does not emphasize the sexual factor in court life, while that of Mme de Lafayette does ('la magnificence *et la galanterie* n'ont jamais paru en France avec tant d'éclat que dans les dernières années du règne de Henri second'), but there is none the less a comparable vision. Indeed, the author of *La Princesse de Clèves* may be indebted to Mme de Motteville for more than a general moral and stylistic attitude. Chapter seven of the latter's memoirs opens with an account of an episode at court in 1643 involving the finding of a dropped letter, and the subsequent tensions arising out of attempts to identify the female writer of it (*6*, 1, pp.135-43), that could have provided the idea of the letter episode that functions so richly in the *nouvelle*, and which has no known source in the annals of the years – nearly a century earlier – during which the events of our text are supposed to be taking place. There is nothing to prevent us from supposing that Mme de Motteville imparted this particular recollection – which, like the rest, remained unpublished until well after her death -- and thus furnished her young friend

with authentic historical material to be creatively fused, as
anachronistically as that culled from chronicles of the Valois reigns,
into the timeless fictional amalgam that is *La Princesse de Clèves*.
Equally, Mme de Lafayette may have had knowledge of the episode
from another source, since the story of the dropped letter is to be
found also in the *Mémoires* of Mlle de Montpensier.[12] In this
version, *two* letters are involved, allegedly from Mme de Longueville
to Coligny and dropped by the latter (they were in reality from the
comte de Maulevrier to Mme de Fouquerolles). In addition, Mlle de
Montpensier mentions another, similar, later episode (in 1658), when
the court was at Fontainebleau, and recounts the attempt made by
Anne of Austria to identify the writer of the (in this case, single)
letter (*8*, III, pp.275-76). But be that as it may, for many of the first
readers of the work, the Valois past was reflected in the Bourbon
present, manifested in the court of the young Louis XIV, so that the
episode concerning the astrologer, for example, would have acquired
resonance from knowledge of the prediction by a contemporary
practitioner of the art that the Queen Mother, Anne of Austria, would
recover from her cancer at the time (the early weeks of 1666) when
in reality she was terminally ill. (This also is mentioned by Mme de
Motteville; cf. *6*, IV, p.419.) But *La Princesse de Clèves* undoubtedly is a work of *fiction*. If, as Mme de Lafayette alleges, the
nouvelle was *really* originally 'des mémoires', who, then, was their
'author'? Which of the characters could possibly have been in a
position to describe the totality of events? Or to comprehend
objectively all the feelings involved? The text is clearly, in its
essentials, a product of the imagination. Surrounded by historical
figures (many of whom – e.g. Saint-André – make appearances in
other fiction of the time), the two crucial characters of Mlle de
Chartres and her mother are not recorded in history at all: they are
invented. Of the other two protagonists, the historical original of one
(Clèves) was a shadowy prince of whom virtually nothing is known,
except that he died (unmarried) just before his twentieth birthday.

---

[12] Bibliography, *8*, I, pp.76 *et seq*. The texts of the letters are given on
pp.76-78.

The other (Nemours – whose *name,* incidentally, carried by a member of a later generation, appears in Mme de Motteville's story of the dropped letter; cf. *6,* 1, p.138) was a notorious playboy of the Valois world, whose sexual conquests were so well known that it could have been argued by the author, had she been attacked by historians on the question of his relationship with a young woman whose existence is not authenticated by history, that he would have been careful not to publicize his failures. And it is through the imagined consciousness of these four figures that the tale is principally mediated. Events are not seen 'murally' (i.e. like a wall-painting) so much as *dramatically* and *psychologically,* and the reader *lives* the events through association with the feelings of the protagonists. The author of *La Princesse de Clèves,* like most novelists who set their writing about human beings in past times, is really interested in human beings in the present (and their possibilities, perhaps, in the future). Her concerns are not archaeological. Mme de Lafayette surely meant, when she said of her text: 'c'est proprement des mémoires', not only that it has the *tone* of memoirs, but also that the moral stresses and strains of its characters, as well as the essential lineaments of the pattern in which they are placed, were manifest in court life of her own day (although never as closely connected as Mme de Motteville, she too had first-hand experience of it), presented as it were in fancy-dress, transposed back into an evocation of a bygone age. After all, the passage quoted claims also that the *nouvelle* is 'une parfaite imitation du monde de la cour et de la manière dont on y *vit*' – in the present tense. History offers a point of departure for one literary way in which the imaginative creative mind can respond critically to its own life, its own emotional situation, or its own fantasies.

4. The Characters

There is a sense, clearly, in which all fiction (and particularly fictional writing with a psychological emphasis) has its source in the mental history of the writer. But even if it is claimed that in any given work all the personages presented through their feelings or thought processes, however partially, 'are' (again, in a sense) the author, the most that this can justifiably be taken to mean is that each personage shows an *aspect* (or aspects) of the author's consciousness, and even then not necessarily consistently, or unaltered. A text may well be rooted in a problematic situation, in a question or questions to which the author knew he did not possess an unequivocal answer. A novel – or a *nouvelle* – of the broad category to which *La Princesse de Clèves* belongs depicts a *world*, and in that world – as in the more general world we all perforce inhabit – the unchanging 'human nature' that I mentioned is manifested as it were by diffusion, shown forth by *characters* in whom it is modified and conditioned by temperament or personality, environment (including upbringing) and experience.

There are four main characters in *La Princesse de Clèves* (although the author also makes excursions into the consciousness of certain minor figures, like the chevalier de Guise, the vidame de Chartres, and Mme de Thémines, in order to support and generalize the patterns of thoughts and emotions of the protagonists): the prince de Clèves, the duc de Nemours, Mme de Chartres, and her daughter. Clèves, we are told (p.37/71), is 'parfaitement bien fait' (i.e. of attractive appearance), 'brave', 'magnifique' (i.e. with a taste for display in dress and ostentatious formality in other aspects of his life-style), and possesses 'une prudence qui ne se trouve guère avec la jeunesse' – a suggestion of precocious maturity, even of sombre calculation. His personality is therefore contrasted from the outset in one essential respect with that of Nemours – Clèves is not particularly amiable. He is also, however, well-intentioned: even if his appreciation of his future wife's modesty (p.42/77-78) is interpreted in the last analysis as self-interest (a modest girl, it may be thought, is less likely to be a source of trouble in the circumstances of life at court), one should not overlook the vein of stubborn idealism that causes him to resist his father's attempt to break the match (p.46/82-83) and to try to clarify the feelings of Mlle de Chartres before the marriage (pp.49-51/86-88) ('ce qui troublait sa joie était la crainte de ne lui être pas agréable, et il eût préféré le bonheur de lui plaire à la certitude de l'épouser sans en être aimé'), nor the importance he attaches to sincerity (p.76/116-17). His unawareness of the limitations of his own nature, however, is total: 'vous m'estimez assez', he assures his wife after her confession (p.123/172), 'pour croire que je n'abuserai pas de cet aveu. Vous avez raison, Madame, je n'en abuserai pas et je ne vous en aimerai pas moins'. But within a few moments, he is accusing her of giving away her picture as an amorous token (p.124/173), within a few days he is trapping her into confirming his suspicions of the identity of her admirer (pp.126-29/175-79), within a few days more he is sending his officer to spy on Nemours and passionately embracing as the truth the least charitable interpretation of the officer's scrupulously incomplete report (pp.154-60/207-15). Clèves is not a conventional 'villain', the hideous husband, the cliché-figure whose whole function is to be an obstacle to happiness. The author's presentation of him as complex and inconsistent is one way in which *La Princesse de Clèves*, to quote Michel Mercier again, 'renverse les règles du jeu'. The reader is being led out of the world of romance into that of reality.

If Clèves is neither perfect nor completely composed of imperfections, much the same can be said of Nemours. Initially, granted, he is presented (p.37/71-72) in terms of the easy superlatives that are part of the stock-in-trade description of the seventeenth-century 'héros de roman'. But this hyperbolic evocation, if it helps to explain the fascination he quickly comes to have for the inexperienced Mme de Clèves' is balanced by notations of attitude and behaviour that are less attractive and help equally to explain why she ultimately rejects him. There are in Nemours disquieting areas of moral ambiguity. If the generality of court ladies is more than aware of his charm ('peu de celles à qui il s'était attaché, se pouvaient vanter de lui avoir résisté, et même plusieurs à qui il n'avait point témoigné de passion, n'avaient pas laissé d'en avoir pour lui'), he himself is not displeased that this should be so. 'Il avait tant de douceur et tant de disposition à la galanterie', as the author puts it with elegant euphemism, 'qu'il ne pouvait refuser quelques soins à celles qui tâchaient de lui plaire'. We have here not only an indication of temperamental proclivity responding to an environment but also a considerable hint of casual amorality, an impression reinforced by the information that 'il avait plusieurs maîtresses [although in the seventeenth century this term does not necessarily imply the carnality of relationship basic to modern usage[13]], mais il était difficile de deviner celle qu'il aimait véritablement' – a hint that is confirmed when we are told (p.60/99) that his attraction towards Mme de Clèves is so intense 'qu'elle lui ôta le goût et même le souvenir de toutes les personnes qu'il avait aimées et avec qui il avait conservé des commerces pendant son absence. Il ne prit pas seulement le soin de chercher des prétextes pour rompre avec elles; il ne put se donner la patience d'écouter leurs plaintes et de répondre à leurs reproches'. High-handed in his sexual imperialism, he is also, not surprisingly, irresponsible – witness the theft of the miniature (p.92/136), which he commits virtually on impulse, and without thought of possible consequences for the woman he claims to love. When care for the heroine's reputation *is* manifested, it is little more than one of the techniques of the experienced predator. Examples of these techniques are not difficult to find: we are told, for instance, that during the illness of Mme de Chartres, 'ce prince trouva le moyen de voir plusieurs fois Madame de Clèves en faisant semblant de chercher son mari ou de le venir prendre pour le mener promener. Il le cherchait même à des heures où il savait bien qu'il n'y était

---

[13] See standard dictionaries of the period like those of the Académie, Furetière, and Cotgrave.

pas...' (p.67/107); there is his statement (p.85/127) to the princess
herself, couched deliberately in general terms but with unmistakable
personal application, that:

> les femmes jugent d'ordinaire de la passion qu'on a pour
> elles... par le soin qu'on prend de leur plaire et de les
> chercher; mais ce n'est pas une chose difficile, pour peu
> qu'elles soient aimables; ce qui est difficile, c'est de ne
> s'abandonner pas au plaisir de les suivre; c'est de les
> éviter, par la peur de laisser paraître au public, et quasi à
> elles-mêmes, les sentiments que l'on a pour elles.

Similarly, we are told (p.86/129) that a little later, modifying his
approach, 'ce prince trouva le moyen de lui faire entendre... qu'il
allait à la chasse pour rêver, et qu'il n'allait point aux assemblées
parce qu'elle n'y était pas', while a few days later still (p.88/131), he
tries to make Mme de Clèves believe, with elegant irony, that an
astrologer has foretold an impossible future for him: '"On m'a prédit,
lui dit-il tout bas, que je serais heureux par les bontés de la personne
du monde pour qui j'aurais la plus violente et la plus respectueuse
passion. Vous pouvez juger, Madame, si je dois croire aux
prédictions"'. It is significant, too, that when the reine dauphine asks
him to repeat this aloud, we are told that 's'il eût eu moins de
présence d'esprit, il eût été surpris de cette demande. Mais [il prit] la
parole sans hésiter'.

The vigorous male is here overlaid by the smilingly submissive
well-bred lover and resourceful courtier. But there are other times,
when we can see clearly the mental operations of this seasoned
sexual campaigner – for example, when the princess, believing
Nemours to be the addressee of the 'lost letter', refuses to receive
him. 'Ce prince', the text runs (p.113/159), 'ne fut pas blessé de ce
refus: une marque de froideur, dans un temps où elle pouvait avoir de
la jalousie, n'était pas un mauvais augure'; and when he does succeed
in his attempt to see her, we are told (p.114/161) that 'l'aigreur que
Monsieur de Nemours voyait dans l'esprit de Madame de Clèves lui
donnait le plus sensible plaisir qu'il eût jamais eu'. Again, we are

told that, having overheard the heroine's confession, 'il trouva de la
gloire à s'être fait aimer d'une femme si différente de toutes celles de
son sexe' (p.126/175), and that, when the 'leak' occurs, 'Monsieur de
Nemours, qui vit les soupçons de Madame de Clèves sur son mari,
fut bien aise de les lui confirmer. Il savait que c'était le plus
redoutable rival qu'il eût à détruire' (p.134/186). However, we are
admitted to his consciousness less frequently, and in general with less
precision, than is the case with the other protagonists. In the main,
the most the reader is vouchsafed of Nemours is a reference to his
'feelings' – see, for instance, the description of him wandering in the
wood at Coulommiers (p.157/211). The few occasions on which we
are told more are either revelations of egocentricity, as in the
passages just cited, or are ambiguous: a good example is his
statement (p.85/127) that 'ce qui marque... un véritable attachement,
c'est de devenir entièrement opposé à ce que l'on était, et de n'avoir
plus d'ambition, ni de plaisirs, après avoir été toute sa vie occupé de
l'un et de l'autre'. True no doubt as a principle, but is it true for him?
Are we to take it that he *believes* what he is saying (he is saying it to
the princess)? Does the author wish us to think of Nemours as a
young man who does not yet understand himself? Another instance
of ambiguity is provided, perhaps, by his conduct towards Mme de
Clèves at the festivities following the proxy marriage of the king's
daughter, at which 'il lui fit voir tant de tristesse et une crainte si
respectueuse de l'approcher qu'elle ne le trouva plus si coupable'
(p.141/194), although on balance this is more likely to be a case of
calculated policy than of genuine remorse, since it follows hard upon
his decision (p.140/192) 'd'attendre ce que le temps, le hasard et
l'inclination qu'elle avait pour lui pourraient faire en sa faveur'. That
his hunter's instincts are still unimpaired is clearly shown by the
unequivocal notation (p.168/224-25) of his attitude shortly before the
final interview:

> Lassé enfin d'un état si malheureux et si incertain, il
> résolut de tenter quelque voie d'éclaircir sa destinée. Que
> veux-je attendre? disait-il; il y a longtemps que je sais
> que j'en suis aimé; elle est libre, elle n'a plus de devoir à

m'opposer; pourquoi me réduire à la voir sans en être vu
et sans lui parler? Est-il possible que l'amour m'ait si
absolument ôté la raison et la hardiesse, et qu'il m'ait
rendu si différent de ce que j'ai été dans les autres
passions de ma vie? J'ai dû respecter la douleur de
Madame de Clèves; mais je la respecte trop longtemps et
je lui donne le loisir d'éteindre l'inclination qu'elle a
pour moi.

The uncertainty surrounding Nemours is none the less charged with
significance, particularly given that our response to the ending of the
tale depends in large measure on our evaluation of what it is that the
princess is rejecting. Clearly, she has by then learnt something, for
good or for ill. But has *he*? He may be no worse that the 'average'
man, but he is no better, either.

If it is possible to think of Nemours as incapable of learning,
the case of the heroine's mother is signally different. We are dealing
here with a character who believes that she *has* learnt (it may be –
depending on how one evaluates the dénouement – to disastrous
effect). Recent critical response to *La Princesse de Clèves* has
included the occasional voice raised in condemnation of Mme de
Chartres as the 'villain' of a text in which, it is more usually agreed,
'villainy' is presented by implication as residing in the basic
constitution of the human ego, and as such *distributed* among the
characters rather than concentrated in a single figure. This view of
Mme de Chartres as 'to blame' for the emotional catastrophe of her
daughter's life depends on the emphasis the reader chooses to place
on some aspects of what the text says about her. Initially, she seems
to be described (p.41/76) in terms of nothing but approval, as a
woman 'dont le bien, la vertu et le mérite étaient extraordinaires',
and the passage that immediately follows selectively expands this
rather vague amalgamated notation of the moral and the social, into a
more detailed characterization that seems to be predominantly moral:

Après avoir perdu son mari, elle avait passé plusieurs
années sans revenir à la Cour. Pendant cette absence, elle
avait donné ses soins à l'éducation de sa fille; mais elle

ne travailla pas seulement à cultiver son esprit et sa
beauté, elle songea aussi à lui donner de la vertu et à la
lui rendre aimable. La plupart des mères s'imaginent
qu'il suffit de ne parler jamais de galanterie devant les
jeunes personnes pour les en éloigner. Madame de
Chartres avait une opinion opposée; elle faisait souvent à
sa fille des peintures de l'amour; elle lui montrait ce qu'il
a d'agréable pour la persuader plus aisément sur ce
qu'elle lui en apprenait de dangereux; elle lui contait le
peu de sincérité des hommes, leurs tromperies et leur
infidélité, les malheurs domestiques où plongent les
engagements; et elle lui faisait voir, d'un autre côté,
quelle tranquillité suivait la vie d'une honnête femme, et
combien la vertu donnait d'éclat et d'élévation à une
personne qui avait de la beauté et de la naissance. Mais
elle lui faisait voir aussi combien il était difficile de
conserver cette vertu, que par une extrême défiance de
soi-même et par un grand soin de s'attacher à ce qui seul
peut faire le bonheur d'une femme, qui est d'aimer son
mari et d'en être aimée.

But there is an element of ambiguity here: is the definition of 'ce qui
seul peut faire le bonheur d'une femme' that of Mme de Chartres
only, or are we to accept it as ours too (in the same way as, we
suppose, the princess accepts it as hers, since there is nothing in the
text to suggest that she does not)? On reflection we may well think
that the considerations involved are only in appearance ethical (i.e.
concerned with good conduct for its own sake), and that they are
really rooted in a care for what is socially acceptable. Indeed, the
next sentence but one reads: 'Madame de Chartres, qui était
extrêmement glorieuse [i.e. socially ambitious], ne trouvait presque
rien digne de sa fille'. This attitude subsequently leads her to try to
negotiate for her daughter a very grand alliance indeed (p.46/83), and
when, this project having come to nothing, she accepts the offer
made by the son of the duc de Nevers, Mlle de Chartres having told
her 'qu'elle l'épouserait... avec moins de répugnance qu'un autre,
mais qu'elle n'avait aucune inclination particulière pour sa personne'

(p.50/87), it is tempting to interpret in the less favourable sense what we are (again) ambiguously told about her mother's attitude towards the match, viz. that 'elle ne craignit point de donner à sa fille un mari qu'elle ne pût aimer en lui donnant le Prince de Clèves'.

At the worst this would seem to indicate a brutal insensitivity. At the best, however, it is no more than evidence of a rather simplistic view of human affection and a lack of judgment, and it is surely for the latter interpretation that the unbiassed reader will opt, faced with the subsequent notation (p.51/88) that Mme de Chartres, noticing ruefully that her daughter is not in love with her fiancé, 'admirait [i.e. was amazed]... que son cœur ne fût point touché, et d'autant plus qu'elle voyait bien que le Prince de Clèves ne l'avait pas touchée, non plus que les autres'. And the author adds: 'Cela fut cause qu'elle prit de grands soins de l'attacher à son mari'. Limited, confused in her values, Mme de Chartres may be, but there is little doubt of the sincerity of her intentions for her daughter's well-being. Certainly not a 'villain', she is in most respects no fool, either: she is percipient enough to notice very early that the princess is interested in Nemours (p.54/92) and that her daughter's decision to absent herself from Saint-André's ball is motivated, not by concern for public opinion, but by fear of what Nemours might think (pp.62-64/102-04). She does her best to present the web of amorous intrigues at court in an unattractive light without indiscreet, counter-productive moralism (pp.55-60/93-99), and her death (pp.67-68/108-09) induces respect not only because it is informed by stoic piety, but because of the attempt she makes to transcend it, on the one hand by a rational analysis of the present situation of Mme de Clèves that shows concern for the latter's future, and on the other by a justification of her own past choice of tactical silence rather than explicit accusation. Mme de Chartres here acquires definitively a stature important enough to carry the weight of an enduring human dilemma. As she says to her daughter: 'il y a déjà longtemps que je me suis apercue de cette inclination; mais je ne vous en ai pas voulu parler d'abord, de peur de vous en faire apercevoir vous-même'. When dealing with the morally immature, does one name a tendency, and thus risk conferring substantive existence upon it, or does one trust in the hope that, unbaptized, it will die of its own accord? Drawing the princess's attention sooner rather than later to her feelings for Nemours might have increased the risk that she would indeed 'tomber comme les autres femmes' (p.68/108).

It may appear paradoxical to devote little more space in this section to the 'chief' character of *La Princesse de Clèves*, through whose consciousness the text largely operates, than to her mother. The reason for this is not, however, as might be supposed, that the princess seems to respect her mother's dying injunction ('souvenez-vous, si vous pouvez, de tout ce que je viens de vous dire') and is therefore, it might be argued, a simple 'product' of maternal indoctrination, her mother's 'creation'. Not the least significant of her subsequent actions is the rejection of Nemours's offer of marriage when she is free to accept it, and this is a contingency no more envisaged by Mme de Chartres than the death of Clèves and the feelings of guilt to which it gives rise. If Mlle de Chartres begins life as, to use the philosopher Locke's term for the human mind before ideas begin to form in it, a *tabula rasa*[14], she becomes Mme de Clèves, a character in her own right, shaped at least partly by her own evaluation of events that transcend her upbringing. The becoming is proportionately much more important than what she might be deemed to be at the outset: her story is one of self-discovery, and it is when she is engaged in discovering herself that she is principally of interest. We need to enquire less into her motivations and psychological lineaments than into those of the three other principal characters because in large measure she explains herself in the text. Even as late as the final rejection of her would-be second husband, we are told (p.176/234) that 'ce lui était une chose si nouvelle d'être sortie de cette contrainte qu'elle s'était imposée... qu'elle ne se connaissait plus'. Certainly, the concept of 'le peu de sincérité des hommes, leurs tromperies et leur infidélité' is formulated for her by her mother, but this is no more than theory until it is illustrated by the first-hand experience of jealousy that reaches its peak of intensity in

---

[14] John Locke (1632-1704). References to the *tabula rasa* are to be found particularly in Book I of the *Essay concerning human understanding* (1690).

the night of mental suffering following the discovery of the lost letter (pp.99-100/145-46). Similarly, if the principle of 'une extrême défiance de soi-même' originates with Mme de Chartres, the agonized rigour with which it is put into practice is a characteristic of her daughter's search for 'des vues claires et distinctes' (p.175/233); moreover, the text states clearly (p.51/88) that 'Madame de Chartres admirait la sincérité de sa fille' – 'la sincérité', that quality ironically and tragically so prized by the princess's husband (p.76/116-17) – 'et elle l'admirait avec raison, car jamais personne n'en a eu une si grande et si naturelle'. The existentially complex reflexions that assail the princess (pp.176-77/234-35) after the definitive interview with Nemours are specific to her – and explicitly stated:

> Elle fut étonnée de ce qu'elle avait fait; elle s'en repentit; elle en eut de la joie: tous ses sentiments étaient pleins de trouble et de passion. Elle examina encore les raisons de son devoir, qui s'opposait à son bonheur. Elle sentit de la douleur de les trouver si fortes et elle se repentit de les avoir si bien montrées à Monsieur de Nemours. Quoique la pensée de l'épouser lui fût venue dans l'esprit sitôt qu'elle l'avait revu... elle ne lui avait pas fait la même impression que venait de faire la conversation qu'elle avait eue avec lui; et il y avait des moments où elle avait de la peine à comprendre qu'elle pût être malheureuse en l'épousant. Elle eût bien voulu se pouvoir dire qu'elle était mal fondée, et dans ses scrupules du passé, et dans ses craintes de l'avenir. La raison et son devoir lui montraient, dans d'autres moments, des choses tout opposées, qui l'emportaient rapidement à la résolution de ne se point remarier, et de ne voir jamais Monsieur de Nemours... Enfin... elle pensa qu'il n'était point encore nécessaire qu'elle se fît la violence de prendre des résolutions.

The subsequent confirmation (p.178/236) of the dismissal of Nemours is motivated not only by a desire for perfection and a moral scrupulousness which could partly, perhaps, be ascribed to her education. It manifests also a longing for quiet, all passion spent, which, temperamental or not, is a direct personal response to lived experience: 'Elle rappelait la mémoire de Monsieur de Clèves, qu'elle se faisait un honneur de conserver. Les raisons qu'elle avait de ne point épouser Monsieur de Nemours lui paraissaient fortes du côté de son devoir et [note the emphasis] insurmontables du côté de son repos. La fin de l'amour de ce prince, et les maux de la jalousie qu'elle croyait infaillibles dans un mariage, lui montraient un malheur certain où elle s'allait jeter'.

We might here, perhaps, ask the question: to what extent is the princess, to use her mother's words when expressing her fears for the future, 'comme les autres femmes'? Is her decision 'unreal'? Some readers, past and present, have thought so. The question will be discussed later, in the conclusion. But for the moment, if we are tempted to think of her as a special creature of authorial fantasy, let us remember the well-documented case from 'real life' of Mme de Lafayette's own sister-in-law, Louise de Lafayette (1615-65), which is comparable in certain essential respects to that of Mme de Clèves. A serious and likeable young woman, according to Mme de Motteville (*6*, I, pp.58-65), Louise attracted the attention of Louis XIII while she was companion and lady-in-waiting to his wife, Anne of Austria. There is no doubt that she and Louis became deeply attached to one another. But at the age of twenty-one, as an alternative to being installed as the king's mistress at the then hunting-lodge of Versailles, she left the relatively permissive court and entered a convent (that of the Filles de Sainte-Marie), subsequently becoming, under the name Mère Angélique, the first superior of an order (that of the Visitation) that she founded at Chaillot. One could also point, for a parallel to the fear expressed by Mme de Clèves (p.173/231) that 'les engagements éternels' do not guarantee the permanence of love (and indeed make its cessation more difficult to bear), to the account given also by Mme de Motteville of the outcome of the ardent pursuit of a Mlle de Boutteville by Châtillon: 'Son mariage... ne fut pas si heureux qu'apparemment il le devait être. Le comte de Châtillon se dégoûta par la possession: il aima une des filles de la Reine, qui n'était pas si belle que sa femme' (*6*, I, pp.230-31). Or there is the case in the 1670s of Mlle de Montpensier and her unfortunate infatuation with the military adventurer Lauzun, who apparently possessed (like Nemours) all the attributes of the 'honnête homme héros de roman', but who subsequently was found to possess feet of clay also. The affair was no secret to the court and society in general, and was certainly known to Mme de Lafayette, who is reported in Mlle de Montpensier's memoirs (*8*, IV, p.241) as having (with her friend Mme de Sévigné) made unfavourable comments on Mlle de Montpensier's intention to marry the man. Perhaps the abdication and retreat of the princesse de Clèves are not so divorced from reality as some would have us believe.

5. Psychology

It may be objected to the last paragraph of the preceding chapter that the evidence adduced to support the claim of *vraisemblance* for the princess's decision relates to the seventeenth century, and that the world has changed. This is indeed so, to some extent. Every human act takes place within a specific, conditioning (although not necessarily *determining*) social situation, which has to be taken into account in our evaluation of that act. Every human decision is therefore in a sense a historical act. In the twentieth century, there is for many women more than one viable alternative to marriage, but in the seventeenth century, in France, there were not many socially acceptable substitutes for 'aimer son mari et en être aimée'. One of the few possibilities would have been the course in fact chosen by the widowed Mme de Clèves, namely a life divided between good works and seclusion. On the face of it, therefore, one might expect her (and perhaps the other characters of *La Princesse de Clèves*) to seem no more authentic to us than the posturing, dated figures that flicker, obeying grotesque histrionic conventions, in early moving pictures. Yet the majority of readers of *La Princesse de Clèves*, however historically separated from the seventeenth century they may be, take in their stride such hurdles of outmoded social idiom as husbands and wives addressing each other respectively as 'Madame' or 'Monsieur', and find these characters to be 'people like themselves'. Why does this happen?

A general answer, of course, is that if the 'world' can change rapidly in the fields of technology, economics, and political and social organization, humans change so slowly genetically and mentally that the process is usually imperceptible except over a long span of generations. In terms of the moral evolution of man, the seventeenth century is only as yesterday. And then, more precisely, it is the seventeenth century that sees the establishment of a view of the

basic nature of the human being that is still one of the normal
working assumptions of many who meditate on the problems of the
individual in European society. In England, for example, Thomas
Hobbes (1588-1679) expressed the view with clarity and vigour:
'The dispositions of men are *naturally* such that... every man will
distrust and dread each other [*sic*]... toward the preservation of
himself'.[15] Or in Holland, the philosopher Benedict (Baruch)
Spinoza (1632-77) put a similar point more abstractly: for him,
everything in Nature (and this includes the human person) manifested
a 'striving, so far as it lies in itself to do so, to persist in its own
being'.[16] But the principle, adequate enough in the world of animals
and less complex organisms which seem to be 'programmed' to obey
their reflexes, is less so when applied to human beings endowed with
a high degree of consciousness and the faculty of judgment, and
aware, in many situations, of the existence of a plurality of
possibilities. How can the individual identify with certainty which of
the 'voices' urging him to differing courses of action is the authentic
voice of his *true* self-interest? Spinoza himself saw the difficulty, and
recommended a method of evaluation that he had taken over from
one of his philosophical predecessors, René Descartes (1596-1650).
This method involved the use of logical analysis, the aim being to
reduce the range of courses of possible action to *clear and distinct
ideas*. This process completed, the victim of a dilemma was then,
theoretically at least, in an optimum position to make a definite
choice. Spinoza's view of the passional pressures on the chooser
would be that a passion also, reduced to a 'clear and distinct idea',
had no greater status than any other 'idea'. For him, as for
seventeenth-century thought in general, the passions were
physiological in origin – they were products of the *senses,* of the

---

[15] From his treatise *De Cive (On the Citizen)*. Quoted by W.G. Moore, *La
Rochefoucauld: his mind and art*, Oxford, Clarendon Press, 1969, p.68. My
italics.

[16] *Ethics*, Part III, Proposition VII. (See Stuart Hampshire, *Spinoza*,
Harmondsworth, Pelican, 1951, p.76.) 'Striving' renders the word 'conatus'
in the Latin text: it could also be translated as 'effort' or 'instinctive
movement'.

body, and a clear and distinct idea could be formed of them as of every other corporeal phenomenon. Mastery comes through reason.

This belief is as implicit in the requests that we still make (in spite of some contra-indications of modern bio-chemistry) that a person should 'control himself', and in the distinction we try to establish, in assessing an individual, between *personality* (which is a matter of given, innate temperament etc.) and *character*, which manifests itself through quality of decision and the way in which the decision is arrived at, as it is in the attempts of Mme de Clèves to understand her feelings, to arrive at 'des vues claires et distinctes' (p.175/233). Our attitude towards behaviour is overwhelmingly still that of the seventeenth century, rooted in what is philosophically speaking a *dualism*, namely the conviction (which was that of Descartes) that there are *two* principles involved in the universe: firstly, that of 'extent', measurable matter, the *physical* (and this includes the animal world), and secondly, that of 'what does the measuring', the mental and spiritual, not subject to the laws governing phenomena belonging to the first category. It is this 'guided missile' concept that explains the *modus operandi*, when trying to determine conduct, of as it were isolating the body as simply the *instrument* of the mind. In the mental mechanisms and the behavioural assumptions of the central character of *La Princesse de Clèves* the reader recognizes his own; and for her, as for the reader, the great question remains: 'What are my true interests? What should I be doing with myself?' It is scarcely necessary to point out the frequency with which the heroine interrogates herself in this way (a particularly representative session, arising out of a sleepless night and the following afternoon spent composing the substitute letter, is described on p.119/167-68). And the same principle holds, negatively, in varying degrees, of the other characters. If, for example, the relationship of her uncle, the vidame, with Catherine de Médicis comes to such a hideous end – 'leur liaison se rompit, et elle le perdit ensuite à la conjuration d'Amboise' (p.118/166) – it is partly because he never *seriously* asks himself precisely this crucial question. And the same is true of the wretched Chastelart, 'favori de Monsieur d'Anville' (p.47/83), whose failure to 'see himself' objectively resulted, history tells us, in his death. The matter is only alluded to in our text in passing, but its first readers would have needed no more than an allusion to sensitize them to the details of his story and to its relevance – following Mary Stuart to Scotland when she became queen of that country, he was charged with *lèse-majesté* for presumptuous sexual behaviour towards his sovereign and hanged, at the age of twenty-four.

It may seem contradictory to speak of 'mental *mechanisms*' when it has just been claimed that, for Descartes and Spinoza, 'things of the mind' are not subject to the laws of the material universe. But not the least interesting distinction of *La Princesse de Clèves* is that it seems to propose a tacit *critique* of one aspect of the attitudes of these two philosophers towards moral freedom. Quite frequently in our text, the 'mental mechanisms' of the characters function in response to stimuli from the material universe (as indeed one would expect), but without being able to prevent those stimuli from continuing to operate as determining factors in conduct: the mind is by implication presented as a tragic observer of its own limitations. Instances are not hard to find. The vidame, for example, admits to Clèves (p.109/155, my italics) that he is aware of the contribution he himself made to the creation of the situation that ultimately leads to his downfall:

> quelque rempli et quelque occupé que je fusse de cette nouvelle liaison avec la Reine, je tenais à Madame de Thémines *par une inclination naturelle que je ne pouvais vaincre.* Il me parut qu'elle cessait de m'aimer et, au lieu que, *si j'eusse été sage,* je me fusse servi du changement qui paraissait en elle pour aider à me guérir, mon amour en redoubla et je me conduisais si mal que la Reine eut quelque connaissance de cet attachement.

And the immediately following sentence suggests that the vidame's failure to control himself is matched by the queen's failure to understand herself: 'la jalousie [a manifestation, in the seventeenth-century view, as has already been said, of the *corporeal* ego] est naturelle aux personnes de sa nation', the vidame reflects, 'et peut-être que cette princesse a pour moi des sentiments plus vifs qu'elle ne pense elle-même'. Clèves apologizes to his wife for having allowed his passion for her to override the bounds of respect and discretion so far as to ask for details of any amorous advances that may have been made to her – and at the same time foresees the likelihood of a recurrence: 'refusez-moi toutes les fois que je vous demanderai de pareilles choses; mais ne vous offensez pourtant pas si je vous les demande' (pp.124-25/174). The princess herself, in the midst of making a firm decision at the crucial point in her history mentioned above (p.119/167-68), paradoxically recognizes the uncertainty of her ability to determine her own behaviour:

> Je suis vaincue et surmontée par une inclination qui m'entraîne malgré moi. Toutes mes résolutions sont inutiles; je pensais hier tout ce que je pense aujourd'hui et je fais aujourd'hui tout le contraire de ce que je résolus hier. Il faut m'arracher de la présence de Monsieur de Nemours; il faut m'en aller à la campagne, quelque bizarre que puisse paraître mon voyage; et si Monsieur de Clèves s'opiniâtre à l'empêcher ou à en vouloir savoir les raisons, peut-être lui ferai-je mal, et à moi-même aussi, de les lui apprendre.

Even allowing for the fact that the last sentence of the passage just quoted has as one of its prime functions the alerting of the *reader* to possible sinister developments, it none the less indicates the heroine's awareness that her own intentions may not be carried out. The ego exists in a context of other egos, and *La Princesse de Clèves* portrays a world in which individual self-preservation can take the form of imposing upon others, it may be at the expense of their peace of mind. This could be equally well illustrated by reference to the scene (pp.92-93/136-37) in which Nemours steals the miniature:

> Il y avait longtemps que Monsieur de Nemours souhaitait d'avoir le portrait de Madame de Clèves. Lorsqu'il vit

> celui qui était à Monsieur de Clèves, il ne put résister à
> l'envie de le dérober à un mari qu'il croyait tendrement
> aimé... Il sentait tout ce que la passion peut faire sentir de
> plus agréable; il aimait la plus aimable personne de la
> Cour; il s'en faisait aimer malgré elle, et il voyait dans
> toutes ses actions cette sorte de trouble et d'embarras que
> cause l'amour dans l'innocence de la première jeunesse.

Manipulation of the beloved, as well as of sexual rivals, enhances the
sense of security of the ego. The paramount consideration, it is
implied, is the survival of the self – a view to be found explicitly
formulated by some other writers of the time, particularly La
Rochefoucauld[17] (a friend of the author of *La Princesse de Clèves*),
who was even prepared to argue that *amour-propre* (as he called it)
was so blindly tenacious that it was capable of ultimate acts of self-
destruction that paradoxically were self-assertive: 'il passe même
dans le parti des gens qui lui font la guerre... il conjure sa perte, il
travaille lui-même à sa ruine; enfin il ne se soucie que d'être'. Even
self-denial can be thought of as a form of self-gratification – a notion
that may not be entirely without relevance to the rejection of
Nemours by Mme de Clèves. And, in the last analysis, the heroine's
confession to Clèves (pp.121-23/170-72) could be interpreted as the
tragic extortion by the dominant husband of a truth that finally kills
him.

For the author of *La Princesse de Clèves*, then, the human *will*
– whatever the scope of human *consciousness* – is not all-powerful. It
would be excessive to claim, however, as some critics have done,
that *La Princesse de Clèves* is therefore 'anti-Cartesian' (i.e. that it
represents a radical refutation of the view of the human creature
offered by Descartes). The work indubitably presents the mind as still
possessing its judicial powers, in spite of its fears that the
maintenance of order may necessitate amputation of the limb that
threatens to be a law unto itself. As Mme de Clèves says of herself

---

[17] François, duc de La Rochefoucauld (1613-80). The statement quoted
appears in the first edition (1665) of his *Maximes*: it does not appear in later
editions.

during the final interview with Nemours: 'les passions peuvent me conduire; mais elles ne sauraient m'aveugler' (p.174/231). The concept of the mind implied by *La Princesse de Clèves* is still basically that of Descartes, but qualified by reflections of the kind to be found in the *Pensées* of another seventeenth-century thinker, the mathematician Blaise Pascal.[18] Pascal is agonizingly aware of the precarious nature of the dominion of human intelligence over the physical universe (which includes the mutinous body), of how easily it can be deflected from its task of observing and assessing. As he reminds us in *Pensée* No 366:

> L'esprit de ce souverain juge du monde n'est pas si indépendant qu'il ne soit sujet à être troublé par le premier tintamarre qui se fait autour de lui. Il ne faut pas le bruit d'un canon pour empêcher ses pensées. Il ne faut que le bruit d'une girouette ou d'une poulie. Ne vous étonnez point, s'il ne raisonne pas bien à présent, une mouche bourdonne à ses oreilles. C'en est assez pour le rendre incapable de bon conseil...

But if, for the author of the *Pensées,* man is – to use an image that occurs more than once in the work – a reed, shaken by the lightest movement of the air, he is none the less a very special reed: 'l'homme n'est qu'un roseau', he writes (No 347), 'le plus faible de la nature, mais c'est un roseau pensant...' Or again (No 348), 'ce n'est point de l'espace que je dois chercher ma dignité, mais c'est du règlement de ma pensée... Par l'espace l'univers me comprend et m'engloutit comme un point, par la pensée je le comprends'. La Rochefoucauld may well be right in claiming that 'la durée de nos passions ne dépend pas plus de nous que la durée de notre vie' *(Maxime* No 5), but the text of *La Princesse de Clèves* is as unequivocal as that of Pascal's *Pensées* in its indication of the two 'orders' of mind and body. Envisaging as she does the possibility of

---

[18] 1623-62. The *Pensées* first appeared, posthumously, in 1670; my quotations are numbered according to the scheme adopted for his edition by Léon Brunschvicg.

defeat – see the passage from p.119/167-68 already quoted – the princess none the less categorically affirms to her husband, during the confession at Coulommiers (p.122/171): 'Je vous demande mille pardons si j'ai des sentiments qui vous déplaisent; du moins je ne vous déplairai jamais par mes actions'. Human strength lies in the knowledge of its own fragility.

6. Love

In the human world of would-be independent, imperialistic egos, what is the function of sexual attraction? What is the nature of what Pascal called in a famous passage 'ce *Je ne sais quoi*, si peu de chose qu'on ne peut le reconnaître', which, as he put it, 'remue toute la terre, les princes, les armées, le monde entier' (*Pensée* No 162)? For him, the phenomenon is clearly rooted in physiology. 'Le nez de Cléopâtre: s'il eût été plus court toute la face de la terre aurait changé'; it is a function of the 'natural' order. Its apparent dependence on reasoned choice is an illusion, and it has nothing to do with what he elsewhere refers to as 'la charité' – *caritas*, love of one's neighbour:

> Mais celui qui aime quelqu'un à cause de sa beauté, l'aime-il? Non, car la petite vérole, qui tuera la beauté sans tuer la personne, fera qu'il ne l'aimera plus. Et si on m'aime pour mon jugement, pour ma mémoire, m'aime-t-on moi? Non, car je puis perdre ces qualités sans me perdre moi... On n'aime donc jamais personne, mais seulement des qualités. (*Pensée* No 323)

Add to this the factor of instability (for Pascal, endemic in the human condition), and love becomes a dangerously shifting value indeed. 'Il n'aime plus', he says, in *Pensée* No 123, of a hypothetical representative man, 'cette personne qu'il aimait il y a dix ans. Je crois bien: elle n'est plus la même, ni lui non plus. Il était jeune et elle aussi: elle est tout autre'. One begins to perceive a deeper level of meaning in the often-quoted claim of La Rochefoucauld (*Maxime* No 136) that 'il y a des gens qui n'auraient jamais été amoureux s'ils n'avaient jamais entendu parler de l'amour'. Pascal puts it more dogmatically and radically still (*Pensée* No 451): 'tous les hommes se haïssent naturellement l'un l'autre. On s'est servi comme on a pu de la concupiscence pour la faire servir au bien public. Mais ce n'est que feindre et une fausse image de la charité. Car au fond ce n'est que haine'. Is love then nothing more than a conceit, a term devised to delude others (and oneself), whilst facilitating the operation of simple lust and the forces of procreation, a tactic in the battle between egos that characterizes the world?

It is in such a world, permeated by illusion, ambition and short-term desire, that Mlle de Chartres is presented precisely as falling in love, an impulsion not the least of the charms of which is that it can appear to be the very antithesis of egocentric, since it seems to involve the unreserved placing of the self at the service of another. But it also – principle of redemption as it may seem to be – presents women in particular with a problem. Women frequently find themselves making statements and asking questions of the kind uttered by the princesse de Clèves in the course of her final interview with Nemours: 'je crois même que les obstacles ont fait votre constance'; 'je vous verrais pour une autre comme vous auriez été pour moi'; 'mais les hommes [which refers in this context specifically to males rather than to human beings in general] conservent-ils de la passion dans ces engagements éternels?' (p.173-74/231). 'I find it impossible', wrote one of the most intelligent of all women writers, George Eliot, 'not to expect some depth of soul behind a deep grey eye with a long dark eyelash, in spite of... experience which has shown me that they may go along with deceit... One begins to suspect at length that there is no direct correlation between eyelashes and morals'.[19] Substitute 'athletic prowess and social grace' for 'eyelashes', and you have an essential aspect of the area of concern of *La Princesse de Clèves*: to what extent is it possible to withstand the solicitations of 'nature' and the pressures of conventional social suitability? At the ball which provides the setting for the first encounter of Mme de Clèves and Nemours, it is

---

[19] *Adam Bede*, Cabinet edition, Edinburgh & London, Blackwood, n.d., I, pp.229-30.

abundantly evident that they are 'naturally' and socially well suited:
'Quand ils commencèrent à denser, il s'éleva dans la salle un
murmure de louanges' (pp.53-54/91). But the fully human needs to
transcend nature, and the individual needs to transcend the narrowly
social.

It is not surprising that a love-story should give no explicit
definition of love – the reading public has its own varied definitions,
compounded of vague prejudices and wishful thinking. This
particular story, the least romantic of romances, presents the reader,
not with definitions, but with *illustrations* of a *range* of conceptions
of love in action, none of them much more encouraging than that of
Pascal, and, leaving him to evaluate them as best he may, invites him
to ponder the problem himself. (A recent critic of *La Princesse de
Clèves* refers to 'the uncertainty of its moral vision', and draws
attention to the fact that it 'inconclusively explores... the virtue of
sincerity, the possibility of happiness in marriage, the proper
recourse of a married woman... in love with another man, the
inevitability that requited love must lead to indifference or jealousy,
and the social, moral, and religious problems occasioned by desires
that are presented as irresistible, adulterous, and destructive, even
when they are neither admitted nor indulged'. This looks like
disapproval. But the critic adds: 'it is from this very lack of sureness
that the power of the work ultimately derives'.[20])

The only immediately attractive one of these conceptions – and
that only initially – is the one the reader meets first, subtending the
view of Mme de Chartres that salvation is attainable through the
putting into action of the slogan: 'aimer son mari et en être aimée'.
The desirability of this objective is patent: stability would thus be
conferred upon a central area of the organization of human life. But it
is soon revealed, in the case of her own daughter, as difficult to
achieve, particularly as the operative criterion is the lamentably
inadequate, negative one of relative lack of distaste for the
prospective husband: 'Mademoiselle de Chartres répondit... qu'elle

---

[20] Anthony Levi, '*La Princesse de Clèves* and the *Querelle des anciens et
des modernes*', *Journal of European Studies*, X, Part 1, No.37 (March
1980), pp.62-63.

l'épouserait même avec moins de répugnance qu'un autre, mais qu'elle n'avait aucune inclination particulière pour sa personne' (p.50/87). (We are given no guidance here, incidentally, by the textually ambiguous nature of the mother's response – 'elle ne craignit point de donner à sa fille un mari qu'elle ne pût aimer en lui donnant le prince de Clèves', which must mean either that the reader is expected to believe that Mme de Chartres is not really concerned for her daughter's happiness or – more likely – that she is the uncritical instrument of her own idealism.) At the other end of the scale is the concept of extra-marital love, enshrined in the story of Mme de Valentinois, inherited by Henri II from François Ier, whom she had persuaded to save her father from the scaffold – 'je ne sais', says Mme de Chartres with euphemistic irony, recounting the matter to her daughter, 'par quels moyens' (p.56/94). The glory and the relative durability of the reign of this royal mistress – it ends only with the death of the king – make it a particularly impressive ambivalent object-lesson for the princess of the possibilities of sexual relationships as a means, accepted by society, to political power – ambivalent because, idealism and morality apart, her mother's account makes it clear that the relationship is informed by recurrent jealousy (for example, the episode involving Brissac, pp.59-60/98-99). Between these two glamorous extremes falls an assortment of notations – the amorous adventures of Henry VIII, the sad account of the career of Mary of Guise, the prophetic evocation of the destiny of Mary Stuart, the attitude towards love of Nemours (pleasure without responsibility), the 'inclination naturelle' (p.109/155) of the vidame for Mme de Thémines *and* Mme de Martigues – all having in common the implied dependence of woman (most unequivocally and dramatically in the case of Anne de Boulen, a clear example of the female as victim). For the most part these illustrations are informed by the principle, explicitly formulated by the vidame (p.109/156), and allied to that of La Rochefoucauld's fifth maxim ('la durée de nos passions ne dépend pas plus de nous que la durée de notre vie'), that 'l'on n'est pas amoureux par sa volonté'. Sex – used, abused, or exploited – is full of enticements but clearly unreliable, and as for 'falling in love', even this phenomenon is rooted in self. The princess

is no exception to the rule: without calculation, since she is a
beginner, she is impressed, however innocently, by the activity of
Nemours, first at the ball, and then during the festivities that
celebrate the marriage of Claude de France (p.55/92). Nemours
exudes vitality, self-confidence, charm. The obeissance of the
heroine's mind towards those qualities is also the first step towards
desiring to possess them by possessing their possessor (and thus
towards a situation in which will appear that autogenous
manifestation of the thwarted ego, jealousy), a process in which
Nemours is, as one would expect, not completely passive, since for
many men, thinking and unthinking alike, self-confidence depends on
continual sexual conquest. 'Il est vrai aussi', we are told in the
paragraph immediately following the passage just referred to, 'que,
comme Monsieur de Nemours sentait pour elle une inclination
violente, qui lui donnait cette douceur et cet enjouement qu'inspirent
les premiers désirs de plaire, il était encore plus aimable qu'il n'avait
accoutumé de l'être...' Conditioned (if not determined) by the urge to
dominate, the ego attracts by 'acting': impelled by awareness of a
potential desirable victim, Nemours gives a spontaneous
performance, playing to an already partially captive gallery. Like all
his performances (and much of what he says or does in the presence
of Mme de Clèves is a performance), this has as its aim not her good,
but her final capitulation. Love in the sense of care for the beloved is
not one of the considerations of this practised operator. He ruthlessly
exploits the signs that she suspects her husband of indiscretion ('il
savait que c'était le plus redoutable rival qu'il eût à détruire',
p.134/186), and manifestations of unhappiness on her part are
welcomed because they indicate disturbance in her ego, caused by
jealousy. 'L'aigreur que Monsieur de Nemours voyait dans l'esprit
de Madame de Clèves', on the morning after the night during which
she had believed the lost letter to be addressed to him, 'lui donnait',
we are told (p.114/161) in a passage that has already been cited, 'le
plus sensible plaisir qu'il eût jamais eu', because he knows that in
this area of human consciousness, reason and intellect can be at the
mercy of the passions – so much so, indeed, that even during the final
interview the heroine's well-grounded decision to reject her suitor is

threatened with reversal by an upsurge of emotion. Initially, she states categorically: 'cet aveu [her confession that she loves him – or, rather, that she is *in love* with him] n'aura point de suite et je suivrai les règles austères que mon devoir m'impose' (p.171/228). This is confirmed and compounded (pp.172-74/230-32) by the evocation of the 'malheurs' that, she argues, would follow marriage to Nemours, the claim 'je crois même que les obstacles ont fait votre constance', and the rhetorical question 'on fait des reproches à un amant; mais en fait-on à un mari, quand on n'a qu'à lui reprocher de n'avoir plus d'amour?' – all of which is a way of indicating clearly that the princess would not marry him even if she owed nothing to her husband's memory. But there then (p.175/232-33) follows a rapid sequence of *emotional* manifestations. Her admission 'je me défie de mes forces au milieu de mes raisons' is immediately used by her lover: 'Monsieur de Nemours se jeta à ses pieds, et s'abandonna à tous les divers mouvements dont il était agité', upon which, we are told, 'Mme de Clèves.... regardant ce prince avec des yeux un peu grossis par les larmes', asks the logically improper question: 'Que n'ai-je commencé à vous connaître depuis que je suis libre, ou pourquoi ne vous ai-je pas connu devant que d'être engagée?' and then forgets her previous (irrevocable) decision so far as to say to Nemours: 'Attendez ce que le temps pourra faire'. The reed-like nature of human volition and the power of propinquity have not often been captured in literature so naturally and discreetly, yet dramatically.

The nature and importance of the passions clearly play a crucial role in *La Princesse de Clèves*. Of all the conceptions of love that figure in the text, overtly stated or covertly implied, only one – 'aimer son mari et en être aimée'– is seen to offer anything like the long-term peace of mind that might be expected as a prime benefit of sexual relationships, and even that, in the case of the princess and her husband, operates less than perfectly, precisely because of the *absence,* paradoxically, from the attitude of one of the partners, of emotional involvement. After the marriage (a marriage presumably consummated, since there is no hint of the situation being otherwise than normal in this respect), Clèves, we are told, 'ne laissa pas d'être

son amant, parce qu'il avait toujours quelque chose à souhaiter au-
delà de sa possession; et, quoiqu'elle vécût parfaitement bien avec
lui, il n'était pas entièrement heureux. Il conservait pour elle une
passion violente et inquiète qui troublait sa joie' (p.52/89). The male
sexual ego demands an answering unconditional voice, participation
in an operatic duo, and is intimately wounded by the absence of
response. Even during the betrothal period, Clèves 'voyait avec
beaucoup de peine que les sentiments de Mademoiselle de Chartres
ne passaient pas ceux de l'estime et de la reconnaissance' (p.50/87),
and his complaint at this lack of passionate feeling is formulated in
terms associated with accusation: 'vous n'avez pour moi qu'une sorte
de bonté qui ne me peut satisfaire'. As for the sexual ego of the
female, this manifests itself no less powerfully, if tacitly, causing the
queen, for example, to allow the vidame to go to his death, and even
Mme de Clèves feels humiliation and anger when faced with what
seems to be evidence that the man whose advances she, as a married
woman of undoubted scrupulous principle, has rightly rejected, has
dared to form a relationship with someone else (pp.99-100/145-46),
or when it seems that he has been guilty of an indiscretion: 'de tous
ses maux', we are told, 'celui qui se présentait à elle avec le plus de
violence était d'avoir sujet de se plaindre de Monsieur de Nemours,
et de ne trouver aucun moyen de le justifier' (p.138/190). And her
reflections continue: 'C'est pourtant pour cet homme, que j'ai cru si
différent du reste des hommes, que je me trouve comme les autres
femmes...' The view of the passions presented by the author of *La
Princesse de Clèves* is not a glibly moralistic one, but *tragic*. The
passions are not seen as of no account, nor as easily surmountable,
but rather as permanent adversaries of the rational will, able, even if
they are ultimately successfully resisted, to damage the victor
irreparably, disguising themselves like the personified *amour-propre*
of La Rochefoucauld (logically enough, since they are the principal
forces through which the ego operates). When Nemours visits the
princess after the death of her mother, at one of the rare moments
when he may *not* be giving a performance, the attraction that she has
for him imposes a paradoxical discretion: 'il s'assit vis-à-vis d'elle
avec cette crainte et cette timidité que donnent les véritables

passions. Il demeura quelque temps sans pouvoir parler' (p.84/126). The notation is ambiguous, certainly. Does it mean that Nemours is genuinely the victim of a 'véritable passion' in an acceptable sense, or that he is conducting himself 'as if'? But in either case, whether his behaviour is genuine or counterfeit, the result of authentic feeling or calculated technique, it impresses Mme de Clèves: a sexual passion is advancing its cause.

It is significant that Mme de Clèves is fully aware of its advance, since after the duke has recovered the power of speech in the episode just referred to, the text states that 'le discours de Monsieur de Nemours lui plaisait et l'offensait quasi également... elle y trouvait quelque chose de galant et de respectueux, mais aussi quelque chose de hardi et de trop intelligible' (p.85/128). As I have said, the attitude of the author towards sexual passion is not moralistic. But it is *moral*: that is to say, the author is concerned with the sources, evaluation and control of decision and action, and the heroine is seen to think of her feelings for Nemours as associated to some extent with guilt – sometimes, as after her husband's death, explicitly (p.164/219-20), and often by implication. This surely is why the episode in which she is represented as approaching most nearly what one could call happiness is the brief idyll during which the substitute for the lost letter is composed from memory (pp.117-18/164-65). It is only then that the heroine's normally mutually exclusive unspoken desiderata – socially (and indeed morally) acceptable nearness to the object of her passion and an absence of blameworthiness in her relations with her husband – are reconciled. But the source of the unfettered elation of the occasion is none the less passional. However ingratiatingly childlike the protagonists' behaviour, it is a function of the sexual ego: 'Monsieur de Nemours était bien aise de faire durer un temps qui lui était si agréable et oubliait les intérêts de son ami. Madame de Clèves ne s'ennuyait pas et oubliait aussi les intérêts de son oncle.' It is only to be a short while (p.136/188-89) before the princess (and her husband) are shown as once again fully conscious of the apparent tragic invincibility of the passions. Having asked his wife, now that her admirer has been identified as Nemours, to conduct herself with particular caution ('Je ne vous le demande point comme un mari, mais comme un homme dont vous faites tout le bonheur, et qui a pour vous une passion plus tendre et plus violente que celui que votre cœur préfère'), Clèves, we are told, 's'attendrit en prononçant ces dernières paroles et eut peine à les achever. Sa femme en fut pénétrée et, fondant en larmes, elle l'embrassa avec une tendresse et une douleur qui le mit dans un état peu différent du sien. Ils demeurèrent quelque temps sans se rien dire et se séparèrent sans avoir la force de se parler' – a mute tableau that sensitizes the reader as much as any explicit statement to the element of tears present at the heart of the human condition. It also represents dramatically the protagonists' realization of the illusory quality of the heroine's naïve hope after her mother's death (p.69/109) that her husband would be capable of transcending the ego ('elle lui témoignait... plus d'amitié et plus de tendresse qu'elle n'avait encore fait... et il lui semblait qu'à force de s'attacher à lui, il la défendrait contre Monsieur de Nemours'). And it is the pressures of sexual jealousy that ultimately kill Clèves. Following the ambiguous report from his officer, 'Monsieur de Clèves ne put résister à l'accablement où il se trouva. La fièvre lui prit dès la nuit même' (p.160/215). The emotional turmoil in his mind makes it difficult for him to interpret the evident concern of his wife in a reassuringly straightforward way ('son affliction... lui paraissait quelquefois véritable et... quelquefois comme des marques de dissimulation et de perfidie', p.161/216), and the relative reconciliation informing his final utterances (pp.163-64/219) – in which, however, he makes no attempt to apologize for misjudging her – is reached only by way of a hurtful, self-regarding and resentful outburst (pp.161-62/217-18) that characterizes the powerful irrationality of the passions:

> Que ne me laissiez-vous dans cet aveuglement tranquille
> dont jouissent tant de maris?... Que ferais-je de la vie...
> pour la passer avec une personne que j'ai tant aimée, et
> dont j'ai été si cruellement trompé, ou pour vivre séparé
> de cette même personne, et en venir à... des violences si
> opposées à mon humeur et à la passion que j'avais pour

vous?... vous connaîtrez la différence d'être aimée
comme je vous aimais, à l'être par des gens qui... ne
cherchent que l'honneur de vous séduire. Mais...
qu'importe... ce qui arrivera quand je ne serai plus...?

Once again the preoccupation of the author is patent – the relentless
tracking down of the manifestations of the ego, the individualizing
force informing our existence that claims, when operating in the
sexual domain, that its life is meaningless without the enjoyment of
the desired object. Sometimes (as in the case of Nemours) it survives
none the less: 'Enfin, des années entières s'étant passées, le temps et
l'absence ralentirent sa douleur et éteignirent sa passion'
(p.180/239). But in the case of the princess, the very intensity of her
emotional dependence on her would-be lover and its centrality in her
existence lead paradoxically not only to the cancellation of this
particular 'game' but to the extinction of the candle itself: 'Madame
de Clèves vécut... dans une retraite et dans des occupations plus
saintes que celles des couvents les plus austères; et sa vie, qui fut
assez courte, laissa des exemples de vertu inimitables'. The
performance of good works, it would seem, is no substitute for the
vital principle. And for us, as well as for the imagined Mme de
Clèves, the question still remains unanswered: 'O body swayed to
music, O brightening glance, | How can we know the dancer from the
dance?'[21]

---

[21] W.B. Yeats, 'Among School Children' (*Collected Poems*, Macmillan, 1967, p.245).

7. Style

Undoubtedly, an important element in the tragic impression made by *La Princesse de Clèves*, the impression of a world in which decision is a product of the interaction of the human condition and the ego, neither of which can be transcended, is constituted by the pattern of events forming the dénouement. However, the sad facts of the text's closing pages do not alone account for that impression. We may agree with Aristotle's dictum that the emotions of terror and pity produced in the theatre by tragedy arise 'from the circumstances of the action itself' (*Poetics*, XIII). No doubt the contention is true of narrative art also. But the action in itself does not automatically cause those emotions to appear. What matters is our *view* of the action: these emotions (among others) need to be *evoked*, the 'circumstances of the action' need to be mediated to the listener or the reader, and this can only be done in narrative art through *language*. Literature *is* (to state the obvious) words, and not the least important factor in our response to *La Princesse de Clèves* is the nature of the words selected (consciously or otherwise) to compose it and the way those words are used – that is to say, the author's *style*.

The word *style* itself has of course come down to us from the Romans. Its Latin ancestor *stilus* – literally a pointed writing instrument – subsequently extended its meaning to signify the *way* in which any particular writer *used* his instrument, and the term 'style' is now commonly utilized to indicate those recurrent distinguishing features of the means of expression manifested in a work of art that enable us to characterize its approach to life, and in some cases to recognize it as the creation of an individual author, with a particular vision of the world. If the *structure* of a work can be thought of as its 'syntax' – the inter-relating of selected material – then the *style* is its 'grammar', the verbal presentation of that material. Frequently, of course, a stylistic characteristic can be no more than a common usage to be found in many works of the same period, and the language of *La Princesse de Clèves* is, understandably, of its time. In the same way as we must remember that although our author uses techniques of the *nouvelle historique* with extraordinary sureness, the *nouvelle historique* itself already existed, we must be prepared to distinguish between an idiom and the effective exploitation of that idiom. The latter-day reader must not allow himself to be over-impressed by locutions simply because they are unfamiliar: one finds here and there, for example, an expression which has been affected by the processes of linguistic evolution – 'd'abord', for example (p.60/99), which meant 'dès le commencement' – and the substitution of 'il ne me haïssait pas' (p.66/106) for 'il m'aimait' is a normal seventeenth-century upper-class euphemism. Similarly, there is an occasional piece of emotive hyperbole that reminds us that our text did not spring to life fully armed like the warriors produced by the dragon's teeth, but is related (however distantly) to the romance, which also used this kind of procedure. The second experience of Nemours at Coulommiers, we are for example told, 'c'est ce qui n'a jamais été goûté ni imaginé par nul autre amant' (p.155/209). 'Style' can refer, however, not only to turns of phrase but also to techniques of presentation in general, and in this broad sense some aspects of the style of *La Princesse de Clèves* have already been mentioned in the chapter on structure; a case in point is Fontenelle's apparently flippant comment at the rival's presence at the confession, namely that he was 'ravi que M. de Nemours sache la conversation, mais... au désespoir qu'il écoute', because this resembled an 'adventure' from a romance (see above p.17).

This is not the only example in *La Princesse de Clèves* of the use of a period fictional convention. The visit to Coulommiers just mentioned includes a description of Nemours, in the setting of some willow-trees and a brook, giving himself up 'aux transports de son amour' (p.157/211) – a scene that derives from the run-of-the-mill pastoral romances – and there is the mention, in the passage preceding the final decisive interview, of Nemours being introduced into the presence of the princess through an 'escalier dérobé' (p.169/225), a 'stage property' that is to be found in the

contemporary heroic novel. Similarly (although on a trumpery
technical level) there is the intrusive heading 'Lettre' (p.97/143), a
publishers' convention that perhaps made its way into the
presentation of narrative fiction from its use as a category title in
anthology volumes. But these 'cliché' elements represent only an
infinitesimal part of the work, and in any case the second and third
examples we have quoted, like the first, have a functional role (the
willows associating Nemours with nature, the 'escalier dérobé'
reinforcing the secrecy of the meeting – secrecy that provides the
princess with an excuse for listening to the duke). They are simply
established ways, lying ready to hand, of attaining one of the main
objectives of the tale, namely the drawing of our attention to precise
and accurate perceptions concerning human emotions and moral
decisions.

Other methods that characterize the texture of *La Princesse de
Clèves* are more distinctive. The first is easy to overlook, but it plays
none the less an important role as a 'hidden persuader' in our
response to the work. It is the straight third-person narration,
inherited ultimately, no doubt, from the tradition of oral story-telling
of the days before the expansion of literacy, but which is used in *La
Princesse de Clèves* with considerable skill to induce belief in what
we are being told. Very early in the text (p.36/70 – only the second
page of the edition to which our quotations refer) the author, having
claimed that 'ce qui rendait cette Cour belle et majestueuse était le
nombre infini de princes et de grands seigneurs d'un mérite
extraordinaire', begins the next sentence with 'Ceux que je vais
nommer...', in the manner of a *historian*. The narrator then
disappears, definitively, without intruding again in this crude 'je'
form, but leaving behind such a powerful assumption of objectivity
that when, much later, doubt is expressed about the heroine's
motivation (the use of 'peut-être', pp.156/210 and 164/220), it seems
to be the scrupulous hesitation of a chronicler who is in two minds
about the matter. The reader is thus left to assess it for himself,
becoming as it were a creative associate of the author in the
exploration of what is accepted as authentic reality. Because of the
author's 'withdrawal', the reader finds himself 'living' the book with

his own imagination.

This withdrawal is paralleled to some extent by the systematic omission of aspects of day-to-day existence, mentioned earlier, in passing, in discussion of the symbolic function of the court. If we think about this matter further, we realize that we are not dealing with a simple blanket exclusion of the physical world, but with an important principle of evaluation and choice. We are given no details of eating or drinking, as already noted, nor is there any mention in general of bodily functions. But there is a reference, when Mlle de Chartres is introduced, to 'la blancheur de son teint et ses cheveux blonds', and we are informed that 'tous ses traits étaient réguliers, et son visage et sa personne étaient pleins de grâce et de charmes' (p.41/77). We are told on two occasions (pp.42/77 and 51/88) that the girl blushes. There is a reference to chairs (p.53/91) and to the sporting activities 'jouer à la paume' (p.55/92 and elsewhere) and 'courre la bague' (p.55/92), as well as to the breaking-in of horses (p.95/140), while the description of the proxy-marriage of Elisabeth de France pays some attention to the colours worn by the participants (pp.140-41/192-94).

All these notations appear in the text for a purpose. They are the occasion, the circumstance or the equipment of important action, they reduce the environment to those aspects of it that provide elements of motivation for the emotions, thoughts or behaviour of the characters (phenomena that they perceive), or that stimulate the reader's imagination (and thus invite him to reflect) by activating recollection of his own social experience. The reader is thus – like the spectator of the contemporaneous classical theatre – held in a world in which his attention is concentrated on the morally and thematically significant. The mention of the tournament colours is particularly illuminating in this respect, not least because its function is explicitly indicated. The text (p.141/194) runs:

> Monsieur de Nemours avait du jaune et du noir. On en chercha inutilement la raison. Madame de Clèves n'eut pas de peine à la deviner: elle se souvint d'avoir dit devant lui qu'elle aimait le jaune, et qu'elle était fâchée

> d'être blonde, parce qu'elle n'en pouvais mettre. Ce
> prince crut pouvoir paraître avec cette couleur, sans
> indiscrétion, puisque, Madame de Clèves n'en mettant
> point, on ne pouvait soupçonner que ce fût la sienne.

But this is not all. A few lines before, we have been told that 'le Roi
n'avait point d'autres couleurs que le blanc et le noir, qu'il portait
toujours à cause de Madame de Valentinois, qui était veuve'. Putting
aside the thought that the author may have intended this to be read,
on a superficial level that hardly ruffles the ruling tone of sustained
seriousness, as a delicately obscene joke, we ask ourselves whether
any importance is to be attached to the fact that black figures among
the colours of both the king and Nemours. The answer is affirmative:
in some of the various schemes of late medieval colour symbolism
(occasionally surviving unmodified to this day – white, for example,
the conventional colour of bridal dresses, is still associated with
purity and chastity), black can signify *constancy* as well as death, and
a good proportion of the first public of *La Princesse de Clèves* would
have been aware of this. (A splendid example of the usage in
sixteenth-century England is to be found in the well-known miniature
by Nicholas Hilliard – now in the Victoria and Albert Museum –
representing a young nobleman – perhaps the Earl of Essex, one of
the favourites of Elizabeth I and allegedly devoted to her – wearing
garments of white and black, which were, precisely, the colours of
the queen herself.)

The mention above of the seventeenth-century French classical
theatre may remind us that in the chapter dealing with the structure of
our text it was suggested that the phases of the action could be
distributed over a 'five-act' schema, and that some other standard
procedures of that theatre were also in evidence – in particular, the
use of confrontation, and of monologue. The second of these formal
elements – the monologue – can also be seen, if more narrowly
considered as language, as having an important stylistic function in
La Princesse de Clèves. One of the ways in which the theatrical
monologue can operate is by 'taking over' the audience, so that a
powerful assimilation (however temporary) takes place between the

sentiments expressed and the sympathies of the listener. Similarly, in our text the use of the first person singular can 'colonize' the reader's consciousness and thus cause him to take as it were an active part in the deliberations of a character.

One mode of utterance frequently met with in French writing of the seventeenth century, and, like the monologue, common to much narrative and dramatic literature, is however – significantly, I think – virtually *absent* from *La Princesse de Clèves*. This is the *maxim*, which may be defined as a short sentence enshrining in abstract, analytical terms a belief about an aspect of the world or the human beings inhabiting it. The maxim is characterized by concision and range of applicability; it is often pithy, sometimes cryptic (although it *can* be not much more than a stylistically attractive, perhaps proverbial, statement of the obvious, or an impressive vehicle for prejudice), and it as often as not expresses a view supposedly held by a majority of the culture-group in which it appears (consider, for instance, the familiar maxim: 'It is more blessèd to give than to receive'). A maxim can reflect an ideology already shared by an author and his public (in which case its use may be thought of as simply one form of preaching to the converted), or it can pre-empt argument, suggesting to a dissenter that his own opinion is invalid because heretical: the maxim can invite the reader to give his assent to – or at any rate consider – a view of the human condition. The maxim has pretensions to universality; the reader may accept with alacrity what is claimed by an author as, let us say, the motivation of a character, if the behaviour of that character is presented as essentially a particular illustration of a general principle of psychological causality, allegedly possessing absolute validity. The seductive prestige of the maxim is considerable, as Pascal surely knew when he claimed that 'tous les hommes se haïssent naturellement l'un l'autre'. Maxims can be very persuasive, authoritatively (sometimes blandly) beating the bounds of an already structured universe.

Given that, as we have seen, certain other dramatic methods can be utilized in prose writing, it is open to the novelist to exploit the maxim also. The author of *La Princesse de Clèves* chooses not to do so. It is a sign, perhaps, of the extent to which she is liberated from the more limiting conceptual commonplaces on which some of the literature of her time reposes, that the work contains only three statements that can be classified beyond dispute as maxims, that they refer, not to social behavioural norms, nor to prescriptive morality, but to basic human psychological characteristics, that they are rather *discoveries* about men and women than pieces of dogmatism, and, moreover, that two of them have a function in the narrative. The first of these two – 'les personnes galantes sont toujours bien aises qu'un prétexte leur donne lieu de parler à ceux qui les aiment' (p.47/83) – plays a small part in the development of the relationship between the heroine and the Dauphine, since it motivates the attempt of d'Anville to convince the king that Mlle de Chartres should be allowed to marry the son of the duc de Montpensier, while the second – 'les paroles les plus obscures d'un homme qui plaît donnent plus d'agitation que des déclarations ouvertes d'un homme qui ne plaît pas' (p.85/128) – indicates unequivocally the growth of equivocal embarrassment in the mind of Mme de Clèves at the attentions of Nemours. The third – 'l'on n'est pas amoureux par sa volonté' (p.109/156) – reveals the wretched self-awareness of the character (the vidame) through whom it is uttered, and, in a deeper and more general way, relates to the subject-matter and theme of the whole work. At the same time, paradoxically, these maxims can cause the reader to recall – and evaluate – his own experience, while inviting him to take up a position *outside* the action and to *judge* the characters concerned from the vantage-point of superior knowledge – and understanding. We are dealing with an author who is sophisticated and open-minded.

The second of the two maxims just quoted manifests two stylistic characteristics – repetition and balance – the perception of which gives the reader aesthetic as well as intellectual pleasure: 'paroles... obscures/ déclarations ouvertes'; 'd'un homme qui plaît/ d'un homme qui ne plaît pas'. *La Princesse de Clèves* generates pleasure of this kind constantly by flattering the reader's intelligence, sometimes – as here – by conducting him through a satisfying verbal (and logical) pattern, sometimes by one type or another of *understatement*, the effect of which, in general, is to imply that he does not *need* to have everything spelt out for him. This may take the form of what seems by implication to be a refusal on the part of the author to describe a phenomenon. For example, the text states cryptically (p.68/109) that the princess, at the end of her final meeting with the dying Mme de Chartres, 'sortit de la chambre de sa mère en l'état que l'on peut s'imaginer'. Again, after the evocation of her fascinated torchlight scrutiny of her admirer as depicted in the 'tableau du siège de Metz' (p.155/209), we are simply told that 'on ne peut exprimer ce que sentit Monsieur de Nemours dans ce moment'. One could cite also the author's claim (p.82/124), the reader having been informed of the report to Mme de Clèves of the change that seems to have taken place in Nemours, that 'aussi ne peut-on représenter ce qu'elle sentit, et le trouble qui s'éleva dans son âme': the reader has been led into a situation in which it is assumed that he will *think*, 'imagining' (as the author indeed says) on the basis of elements of his own experience.

A comment of a related kind may be made on another form of understatement that occurs here and there in the text. This is the apparent hesitation of the author (briefly touched on already in passing) in ascribing motive or imposing explanation, a hesitation that is always only apparent, and varies in degree. Having told us that the princess has had taken to Coulommiers the group of paintings that includes the representation of the siege of Metz, and that among the warriors figuring in the latter is Nemours, the author adds the comment: 'c'était *peut-être* ce qui avait donné envie à Madame de Clèves d'avoir ces tableaux' (p.152/205, my italics). Similarly, a little later, during the episode of the pavilion, the princess is presented as being *perhaps* in two minds about confirming her impression of having seen the duke: 'elle eut envie plusieurs fois de rentrer dans le cabinet et d'aller voir dans le jardin s'il y avait quelqu'un. *Peut-être* souhaitait-elle, autant qu'elle le craignait, d'y trouver Monsieur de Nemours' (p.156/210). And after the death of Clèves when she refuses, not only to see anyone, but even to be informed of the identity of callers, '*peut-être*', we are told, 'que ces ordres si exacts étaient donnés en vue de... Monsieur de Nemours' (p.164/220).

The examples composing this second group of pieces of understatement have a common characteristic: an element of irony (since the author's 'uncertainty' is assumed). Elsewhere in the text, irony is sometimes less covert. One clear instance (already referred to in another connection) is the parenthetical remark of Mme de Chartres when recounting to her daughter how Mme de Valentinois successfully interceded with the previous king to save her father's life, namely: 'je ne sais par quels moyens' (p.56/94). The implication, given what we are told elsewhere – and what is common knowledge from other, historiographical sources – is that those 'means' were sexual. Another instance is provided on the first occasion when the princess fails to honour the agreement to inform Mme de Chartres of any amorous propositions put to her. Nemours having made it discreetly plain that he finds her attractive, 'elle ne se trouva pas la même disposition à dire à sa mère ce qu'elle pensait des sentiments de ce prince qu'elle avait eue à lui parler de ses autres amants; sans avoir un dessein formé de lui cacher, elle ne lui en parla point' (p.61/100). Faced with this kind of perceptively 'objective' notation, the reader makes the intended evaluation, becoming in effect an accomplice of the author.

Understatement, lined with irony or not, is perhaps the principal tonal key to a stylistic appreciation of *La Princesse de Clèves*. It is a very *classical* text. All the instances of understatement quoted possess, by definition, a considerable degree of restraint, and indeed, the whole text is marked by restraint, by that kind of elegant terseness often met with among educated people who know one another, that leaves a great deal unsaid because a literate and sensitive companion will understand what is at issue and will need in essence not much more than facts and selectively powerful hints in order to activate his own experience of the sector of the human world that is under scrutiny. The author's statement of the lack of emotional response by the heroine to her husband's nuptial ardour is a model of civilized compression: 'Monsieur de Clèves ne trouva pas que Mademoiselle de Chartres eût changé de sentiment en changeant de nom' (p.52/89). And the account given to the princess by her mother of how the king's mistress came to transfer her affections from François Ier to Henri II has all the apparent simplicity and ironic negligence of conversational narration: the late king, says Mme de Chartres 'n'avait pas la même tendresse, ni le même goût pour son second fils [as for the recently deceased dauphin]... il ne lui trouvait pas assez de hardiesse, ni assez de vivacité. Il s'en plaignit un jour à Madame de Valentinois, et elle lui dit qu'elle voulait le faire devenir amoureux d'elle pour le rendre plus vif et plus agréable. Elle y réussit comme vous le voyez...' (p.57/95). It could be argued that since this passage, like so much else in the early part of the work, purports to be the transcription of, precisely, a conversation, the tone is accounted for by straightforward 'realism'. But the same tone informs areas of the text where there is no question of conversation between characters: 'si Madame de Clèves', says the narrator, of the heroine's reaction to the two-stage report that Nemours is in love, and with a married woman who can, the princess realizes, only be herself, 'avait eu d'abord de la douleur par la pensée qu'elle n'avait aucune part à cette aventure, les dernières paroles de Madame la Dauphine lui donnèrent du désespoir, par la certitude de n'y en avoir que trop' (p.132/183). The density and concision of passages like this compel admiration of a writer who possesses not only humane comprehension of mental anguish, but the linguistic skill needed to urge the reader towards clear and distinct perception of one of the enduring and central problems of our emotional and moral condition. Whether, however, accession to lucidity is enough – that is, whether the attempt of Mme de Clèves to acquire clear and distinct ideas, and then to apply them to her own situation, brings her happiness – is another matter, and needs to be discussed further.

8. Conclusion

To describe a chapter of a discussion of a work as a 'conclusion' might be taken to imply that it is intended to pronounce definitively on its meaning. Such a hope would however take little account of one important characteristic of texts that are products of the imagination. All tales are on one level *specific* – that is, they recount the adventures, endeavours, conflicts, defeats of x or y, who possess individual lineaments, but if these tales survive – and indeed, if they make an initial impact – that is because they are also *symbolic*, carrying within them elements of, for example, situation, that refer the reader to his own life and emotional structure, since he shares with the characters (and the author) elements of a common humanity, the kernel of which continues in the species – at least in similar cultures – from generation to generation. A work of literary art is a fabulation of essential (although perhaps in some cases only potential) experience, and it does not necessarily furnish answers to the questions that it may raise, any more than the participant in a real-life event is of necessity provided, by the simple fact of his participation, with the resolution of dilemmas that may be manifested in that event. A work of literary art sensitizes, raises the level of the consciousness of its public, but it does not necessarily solve problems. And although the reader, on reflection, may perceive what the problems are (be they psychological, moral, social, political, philosophical) that are embodied in a particular text, the text itself may be cryptic in its presentation of those problems.

This is particularly so in the case of *La Princesse de Clèves*, since its author exercises restraint, not only in the choice of language, but also in the communication of information and in the provision of aids to interpeting what *is* communicated. The very end of the narrative is a case in point. The last page of the work (p.180/239) leaves us with a vision of Nemours

> aussi accablé de douleur que le pouvait être un homme
> qui perdait toutes sortes d'espérances de revoir jamais
> une personne qu'il aimait d'une passion la plus violente,
> la plus naturelle et la mieux fondée qui ait jamais été...
> Enfin, des années entières s'étant passées, le temps et
> l'absence ralentirent sa douleur et éteignirent sa passion.
> Madame de Clèves vécut d'une sorte qui ne laissa pas
> d'apparence qu'elle pût jamais revenir. Elle passait une
> partie de l'année dans [une] maison religieuse et l'autre
> chez elle; mais dans une retraite et dans des occupations
> plus saintes que celles des couvents les plus austères; et
> sa vie, qui fut assez courte, laissa des exemples de vertu
> inimitables.

These closing sentences, at first sight, seem clear enough. But if the
language is limpid, the intention is less so. What are we to make of
the characterization of the duke's passion as 'la plus naturelle et la
mieux fondée qui ait jamais été'? 'Naturelle' it may well be, in a
particular sense: both Nemours and the princess are physically
beautiful, 'naturally' well matched, and a mutual attraction of this
kind is difficult to resist. But 'la mieux fondée'? (The 'qui ait jamais
été' we can dismiss as conventional hyperbole.) In whose eyes would
this passion be unequivocally acceptable, justifiable? In those of the
general run of society, perhaps. But the notation is closely followed
by the evocation of the extinction of passion by time. By placing the
second statement close to the first, the author in effect converts what
by itself might be taken to be not much more than a vague cadence –
a commonplace sad ending – into the preparation for a sternly
uncompromising perception of one of the limits of the human
condition, and the reader is thereby ushered from the level of
sentimental idealism to that of brutally observed reality, in which
even 'la passion... la mieux fondée' is only of relative permanence.
But was this deliberate? (In addition, it is possible to take the 'mieux
fondée', rather more subtly, as 'auto-evaluation' – that is, as

representing the lover's subjective view of his desire for Mme de Clèves.)

Similarly, in the last sentence of all, it is open to the reader to interpret the shortness of the heroine's life after the rejection of Nemours as a result of that rejection. No doubt the majority of readers, their emotions vicariously involved in the story, do so interpret the notation. But we should not forget that we *are interpreting*. There is no grammatical subordination in the sentence as written – the clause 'qui fut assez courte' is a parenthetical co-ordinate, and does not *necessarily* indicate the effect of a cause. Are we dealing with a negligent author, writing, perhaps, in a hurry? Or we might ask, again, whether this uncertainty was intended. Does the author know as well as we that the reader cannot escape the need to interpret when responding to a work of the imagination?

To ask 'Where is the author in all this?' is to put a question that cannot satisfactorily be answered. Even if the author of our text were alive today and willing to be interviewed, we would be unlikely to profit from the exercise. Writers use their writing not only to celebrate life (if, in some cases, at all), but also to incarnate their *doubts* about life, and in the latter circumstance, as the author of *Madame Bovary* put it, nearly two hundred years after *La Princesse de Clèves*, 'la bêtise consiste à vouloir conclure'.[22] It may well be, as another novelist has claimed, that the writing of fiction is a means a writer has of concealing something from himself.[23] But we have no reliable way of identifying what that might have been in the case of the author of *La Princesse de Clèves*. Authorial interventions in the narrative, it might be thought, could perhaps give us clues, but I have found only three of these, and none is of much use to the reader in forming an opinion of the author's personal attitude to the matter in hand. The first is the presentation of the moral atmosphere at court as 'très dangereuse pour une jeune personne' (p.45/81). The second is the ironic remark (p.55/93) that 'Madame de Clèves... était dans cet

---

[22] Gustave Flaubert, in a letter (4 December 1850) to Louis Bouilhet (*Correspondance,* Conard. 1926-33, II, p.239).

[23] Doris Lessing, *The Golden Notebook,* Granada Publishing (Panther), 1979, p.232.

âge où l'on ne croit pas qu'une femme puisse être aimée quand elle a passé vingt-cinq ans'; and the third is the comment on Mme de Clèves after she has read the lost letter (p.99/145): 'il lui semblait que ce qui faisait l'aigreur de [son] affliction était ce qui s'était passé dans cette journée, et que, si Monsieur de Nemours n'eût point eu lieu de croire qu'elle l'aimait, elle ne se fût pas souciée qu'il en eût aimé une autre', and the author adds: 'mais elle se trompait elle-même; et ce mal, qu'elle trouvait si insupportable, était la jalousie...' All three interventions have a technical function, and reflect, no doubt, a straightforward attempt to confirm the reader in his impression that the tale he is embarked upon concerns the emotional development of a young woman who is initially immature. There is nothing to prevent the reader from speculating about the age and experience (and sex) of an author who adopts such a stance, but speculation of this kind is idle: our attention should be focused, to use the terms of the allusively rich title of a volume of essays by the American critic Edmund Wilson,[24] less on the author's wound than on his bow. (The reference is to Sophocles's tragedy *Philoctetes*, in which one Greek warrior – Odysseus – convinces another – Philoctetes himself – that he must leave the island of Lemnos on which he has been confined because of the stench of his festering wound, and rejoin his comrades, because without the magic bow of Apollo which he possesses they will be unable to defeat the Trojans. The application of the story to the phenomenon of the artist in society is plain. However sensational the accidents of his life may be, however interesting, to transpose the image of the wound into psychological terms, the neuroses in which his vision may be rooted, they are ultimately of trivial importance compared with the re-presentation of life in his work, which helps us to perceive reality. What matters is the quality of the fiction, not the clinically recorded case-history of the maker of the fiction.)

   We cannot be certain what the intentions of the author of *La Princesse de Clèves* were, not only in the passage just examined, but

---

[24] *The Wound and the Bow*. Cambridge (Mass.), Riverside Press, 1941, pp.272-95.

in the work as a whole. It could, for example, be the case that it was intended to be taken as the account of a nearly disastrous infatuation. The text will without difficulty bear that interpretation, among others. Sexual activity can easily be generated between individuals who would find it difficult to *live* together for more than a few days, but who none the less – such is their lack of self-knowledge and the strength of the ego – dignify their mutual attraction by the status-term of 'love'. Undeniably, the princess and Nemours find each other attractive. Equally undeniably, the moral potential of the duke as a permanent partner is uncertain, to say the least. Mme de Clèves herself does not mince her words in this matter, telling him plainly to his face during the final interview: 'je crois même que les obstacles ont fait votre constance' (p.173/231), and referring disparagingly, in an evocation of her dead husband, to 'la différence de son attachement au vôtre' (p.174/232); as George Eliot saw, 'there may be good reasons for choosing not to do what is very agreeable' (*Middlemarch*, chapter 2). Also, there is no hint in the text that the institution of marriage itself does not work by definition. The arranged marriage, a historical characteristic of the seventeenth century (and of those preceding it, and still not totally defunct even in the twentieth), is certainly likely to raise emotional and moral problems, but even an arranged marriage can turn out well. By inference, the marriage (arranged or not) of Mme de Chartres was not unhappy – unless here too we are being unwittingly misled by a *careless* writer who did not take into account what the reader might make of an absence of positive indication to the contrary (p.41/76). And in everyday reality an amalgam of the amiability of Nemours and the reliability of Clèves is not beyond the bounds of possibility. Or is it? Could it be that the principal aim of our text is precisely to make us aware of the dangerous idealism of the programme 'aimer son mari et en être aimée', and to remind us that perfection is not of this world? We should not forget that in seventeenth-century France the moral assumptions of the great majority of the population were, *grosso modo*, those of Catholicism, rooted in the notion of logically necessary human imperfection. Viewed from this angle, the 'défiance de soi-même' (p.41/76) urged on Mlle de Chartres by her mother is not an abnormal recommendation; on the contrary, it could be thought of as a routine approach to confessional self-knowledge. However, if we give some special weight to the 'extrême' that qualifies the 'défiance', the door to yet another possible interpretation begins to open. Are we perhaps to take it that the heroine's acquisition of independence of decision is too inflexibly conditioned by her unusual upbringing? Are we being invited to think of her rejection of Nemours as a 'warning' to us – that is, is it not at least possible that the suggestion is being made that the optimum final course of action for the princess would have been to accept the human material offered and to make what she could of it? Has she properly understood what her true interests are? Is the importance that she attaches to her 'repos' (p.175/232) really a disguise for lack of vitality?

Certainly it could be argued that the 'vues claires et distinctes' (p.175/233) to which the heroine successfully aspires are depressing in their clarity and heartbreaking in their distinctness, making no reference to faith or providence. Indeed, from time to time in the history of critical response to *La Princesse de Clèves* it has been commonplace to note the absence from the text of any mention of confession or priestly counsel, an omission that could well be of significance. In spite of what has just been said about official Catholicism, it is patent that the world as presented by our author is not informed by a transcendental design or dependent on, philosophically speaking, a final cause. No more than in the world as seen by Spinoza is there any metaphysical *a priori* assumption of what men and women 'should' be doing with their lives: the events of *La Princesse de Clèves* take place in a world in which principles like 'aimer son mari et en être aimée' are severely disadvantaged by 'l'ambition et la galanterie' (p.44/80). It is a violent and anarchic world, in spite of the political order imposed upon it by its leaders and the conventional linguistic restraint of its members. Very few of the first readers of *La Princesse de Clèves* would not have been at least subliminally aware, as they transposed themselves back in imagination (however intermittently), of such stigmata of the later period of the Valois kings as the massacre of Saint Bartholomew.

And the tensions aroused by the competitive ego, better contained *politically,* no doubt, in 1678, were self-evidently still the same in essence if not in form. Indeed, political containment may well have sharpened awareness of their social and sexual manifestations. With this possibility in mind, it is instructive to compare, however crudely, an essential aspect of the vision of *La Princesse de Clèves* with that of another great work of fiction that had achieved fame with the discerning seventy years earlier, not long after the end of the so-called Wars of Religion. This is *L'Astrée,*[25] by Honoré d'Urfé. D'Urfé had actually fought in the wars, but his work is virtually unmarked by manifestations of violence. On the contrary, this long pastoral romance, set supposedly in the fifth century, in a charmingly mythical Gaul, is characterized by an undertone of belief in the healing power of the union of the sexes, in their compatibility, of faith in the possibility of their reconciliation; and the less acceptable traits of the male sex as it is presented in *La Princesse de Clèves* are all concentrated in the person of one 'bad' shepherd, Hylas, a separate figure, easily identifiable and defeatable. Reading *La Princesse de Clèves* after *L'Astrée* is like moving from an allegory of purgatory (whence it is possible to rise to paradise) to an image (albeit cool and glamorous) of hell, paradise lost. One must not overgeneralize from impressions of this kind; we have to do here with two markedly different authors, and pluralism in attitudes towards relations between the sexes is clearly as much a fact of life as in economic or political arrangements. But the reader who does submit himself to these two texts in chronological order, and who has been struck by what may justifiably be called the *optimism* of *L'Astrée*, is likely to be equally struck in *La Princesse de Clèves* by a very different tone, which he may think of as *pessimistic.* Behind our text, he may think, there lurks a moral discouragement, one of the more usual causes of which, philosophically speaking, is an inability to escape the fascination of determinism.

As we have in part seen earlier, there are passages here and

---

[25] *L'Astrée* began to appear in 1607. An adequate impression of its flavour may be gained from the version (extracts) published in the '10/18' paperback series (Union Générale d'Editions).

there in *La Princesse de Clèves* which might imply a deterministic conception of the world, notations which could be taken to indicate the importance – perhaps the dominance – in human destiny of 'gifts of nature', temperamental as well as more obviously corporeal, over the distribution of which the individual has no control, but the presence of which can inform or modify decision and conduct. The 'humeur ambitieuse' of the queen (p.35/69), the 'beauté... funeste' of the king's daughter (p.36/70), the high social pretensions of the heroine's mother (p.41/77), the 'cœur très noble et très bien fait' of the princess herself (p.49/86), which helps to bring about the confession, the personal graces of Nemours (p.55/92), the lack of initiative of the prince's officer during his mission to Coulommiers (p.154/208), the recognition by Clèves on his deathbed that passionate love is not a matter of choice (he says to his wife: 'Je vous prie que je puisse encore avoir la consolation de croire que..., *s'il eût dépendu de vous*, vous eussiez eu pour moi les sentiments que vous avez pour un autre', pp.163-64/219; my italics), and, lastly, and perhaps critically, since it is not only affected by the decision to renounce but itself then aids the maintenance of the decision, the state of the heroine's health (p.179/237-38) – these notations all function, in varying degrees, as factors in a moral environment.

This, however, in sum, is surely only at the most partial, sporadic determinism, a selective collocation of phenomena that are not substantial enough (nor insisted upon enough in the text) to provide a body of evidence from which to deduce a *system*, in which *all* actions are pre-determined in a pattern reducible to the operations of a machine, and which could satisfactorily explain the totality of the work (except perhaps as the account of a very special case – and if it were that, we would hardly respond to it as we do). It would be less unacceptable, perhaps – more fashionable, certainly – to argue that what may be seen as the pessimism of *La Princesse de Clèves* is rooted in a view of life that, to use modern terminology, could be called *absurd*. It might be possible to interpret the work as a statement about the human predicament in a universe thought of as *random* or *contingent*, and in which the sexes have incompatible desiderata, women in particular seeking permanence, the absolute, in a world in which, to quote a notorious line of Samuel Beckett in *Waiting for Godot,* human beings 'give birth astride of a grave'.[26] It has already been suggested that the system of nature and the system of human values are not integrated. May it not also be that in the human world itself, by analogy, the two sexes are similarly not (completely) integrated?

The inclusive totalitarian seductions of this approach should, however, in my view, be resisted. Neither the 'determinist' nor the 'absurdist' hypothesis, however superficially attractive they may be, is really acceptable historically. The notion of a middle or late seventeenth-century French writer positing a universe in which the individual human will had no active function is highly improbable, since he would have been working from a simpler, more rational human model than any of those suggested by latter-day science. It may be argued that Pascal attacks reason: certainly, but the target of the attack is the limitations of run-of-the-mill *egocentric* reason, and is made in the service of a higher, transcendent rationality. Similarly, if La Rochefoucauld reveals the chaos attributable to the machinations of *amour-propre*, his revelations are in the nature of a salutary warning, a tacit invitation to self-examination. What is more likely is that *La Princesse de Clèves* is predominantly informed, not by 'determinism', nor by 'absurdism', but – characteristically 'classically' – by dispassionate contemplation and scrutiny of what is. Rather than what may be suggested by any of the 'pessimistic' stances, the work seems to propose a cautious, rational, sceptical assessment of a particular attitude, well established by the last third of the century, towards the relation between the will and the passions, an attitude typified by aspects of the writings of Descartes and, in imaginative literature, by the plays of the middle period of Corneille, and which perhaps seemed to Mme de Lafayette, it may well be in the light of experience, excessively and therefore dangerously over-optimistic. But be that as it may, our author, as Anatole France[27] once wrote of her, 'n'a pas dit son secret'.

---

26   Act II (Pozzo) (Faber, 1959, p.89).

27   Edition of *La Princesse de Clèves* (Conquet, 1889), préface.

The principle that 'keeping one's secret' is of the essence of the truly interesting writer is particularly applicable to the seventeenth century of France. Part of the response to a classical work of art is, precisely, an attempt to 'read the riddle', since the great classical imaginative authors rarely do more than hint at their own attitude towards the situations expressed in their text. The dominant ethical thinking that emerges from them, however, is clearly subtended none the less by a preoccupation with the capacity of the human being to survive the threat to himself or the community (or both) that is potentially present in the ego, although individual assessments of this capacity – and of the gravity of the threat – vary. For Corneille, the ego can be the source of greatness, manifesting itself victoriously in action (often political) or, defeated, in stoical glory, and, as far as love is concerned, if relationships are sometimes brought to nought, it is through the agency of imperatives that, ultimately *accepted* by the protagonists, are not of their devising: there is nowhere to be found in the work of Corneille, expressed or implied, a distrust of love itself. For Molière, not surprisingly, since he is working in the comic register, disorders traceable to the ego can be cured (or at least, their social effects can be contained). For Racine, on the other hand, the ego – usually, in his plays, the sexual ego – is the tragic channel through which the gods dispense disaster. There is no doubt general agreement that, however much the mental *modus operandi* of the heroine of *La Princesse de Clèves* may recall the world of Descartes (the constant search for 'des vues claires et distinctes') and of Corneille, the overall impression left to the reader of the nature and importance of the passions is nearer to that associated with Racine. But to point out the diversity of what one could call the philosophical associations of *La Princesse de Clèves* is not to allege that it is aesthetically unsatisfactory, vitiated by shifts of focus, the manifestation of an intermittent vision. It is clearly the product of a powerful organizing intelligence. No doubt it is not the first prose fiction in which a woman analyses herself. But it is the first of any stature in which that analysis goes beyond the first stage, namely, simple delineation of feeling: in *La Princesse de Clèves*, feelings, over and over again, are systematically linked to actions as causes to effects or effects to causes. Similarly if, in the field of structure, there are orthodox romances written before *La Princesse de Clèves* in which attempts are made to integrate digressions (for example, the *Alcidamie* of Mme de Villedieu, published in 1661), the relating of them to their main subject is haphazard. It is *La Princesse de Clèves* that successfully pioneers the use of organic episodes that can function as proleptic analogues. *La Princesse de Clèves* is, in addition, undeclamatory in its use of language, undogmatic and undidactic in its perceptions. It is undemonstratively sophisticated and modern in its artistic procedures. The very mixture of associations of the work is to be evaluated as evidence of complexity, perhaps of *per*plexity, but certainly not confusion. The author is not a *naïve* writer – certainly not in the sense given to the adjective in the eighteenth century by Friedrich Schiller in a celebrated study[28] and more readily illustrated for English readers, perhaps, by the similar use made of it more recently by Isaiah Berlin[29] in his essay on 'The Naïveté of Verdi', in which he claims the composer of *Rigoletto* as the last European working in the field of opera to possess an unreflecting, spontaneous sense of ethical right and wrong. There is no clear indication at the end of *La Princesse de Clèves* (nor, indeed, anywhere else in the narrative) of the 'rightness' or 'wrongness' of the actions of the princess – whatever may be said or implied about the moral level of representative activities in the society in which she lives. Flaubert's excitingly attractive view of the relation of the creative writer to his work ('comme Dieu dans l'univers, présent partout, visible nulle part'[30]) is applicable to *La Princesse de Clèves* only with the qualification that our 'god-author' has not simply given readers free will to respond as they think fit to the world re-created in the text, but also fluctuates in his own response to the creatures of that world. It is surely no accident – no piece of 'careless' writing –

---

28 *Über naïve und sentimentalische Dichtung*, 1795.

29 *Against the Current*, O.U.P. (paperback), 1981, pp.287-95.

30 *Correspondance* III, pp.61-62. There is another formulation of the notion in *Correspondance* I, p.164. Flaubert may well be paraphrasing Schiller, who had said something similar in the essay mentioned above.

that Mlle de Chartres is warned by her mother on her arrival at court: 'si vous jugez sur les apparences en ce lieu-ci, vous serez *souvent* trompée' (p.56/94, my italics). 'Souvent', *not always. La Princesse de Clèves* is no incondite effusion: the 'souvent' is of the essence, setting up in the heroine's mind – and in ours – the idea of the necessity of personal judgment in individual cases, and of the *difficulty* of judgment. Manifestly, the creator of the universe of *La Princesse de Clèves* perceives the tensions caused by the existence in us of apparently incompatible solicitations – the tension, in particular, between some of the immediate impulsions of the ego and the desirability of identifying the real, transcendent needs of the ego. The alternations set up by this awareness, which permit the author to move from sympathy to ironic detachment and back again, can hardly be alleged as an imperfection.

Afterword

It may seem illogical to follow a 'Conclusion' – however inconclusive – by any statement but a modification. But something remains to be said. The question 'Where is the author?' having been asked, scruple demands that we also ask '*Who* is the author?', since the ascription of our text to Mme de Lafayette rests, strictly speaking, on a presumption (albeit strong), that has occasionally in the past become a matter of contention. There is no *proof* that she wrote *La Princesse de Clèves* (although, as we have seen, there are references to the work in her letters and those of correspondents, and some of those references can without difficulty be interpreted as veiled hints). *La Princesse de Clèves* originally appeared anonymously, and was not published under the name of Mme de Lafayette until after her death, and some critics have fastened on this lack of certainty, claiming variously that she must have received technical assistance from a professional writer of *nouvelles* called Segrais (as may well have been the case for the romance, *Zayde,* which appeared in 1670), that it was predominantly from the pen of her friend La Rochefoucauld, or that it was the product of group activity by a number of society *literati.*

Something could be said for all these attitudes, but none of the arguments put forward is any less circumstantial than those advanced in defence of the conventional point of view. For example, it has been claimed that the work is probably mainly by the author of the *Maximes* because, although the text contains only a few examples of the form, it contains in addition a number of what, it is maintained, are 'notional' maxims, padded out and represented by incidents that 'illustrate' them.[31] It has also been claimed[32] that the aforesaid

---

[31] Cf. the *Tableau de la littérature française: XVIIe XVIIIe siècles* (éd. André Gide), Gallimard, 1939, article on La Rochefoucauld by Jacques Lacretelle.

[32] Fernand Baldensperger. 'Complacency and criticism: *La Princesse de*

literary team (of which, perhaps, it is admitted, Mme de Lafayette might have been a member) cobbled together *La Princesse de Clèves* at the instigation of its publisher, Claude Barbin, who had already been responsible for printing and marketing *Zayde*. Barbin, the theory states, was jealous of the success of the yet earlier *nouvelle* (*La Princesse de Montpensier*, 1662) brought out by another publisher (Thomas Joly), and was ambitious to exploit the success of a short work, *Les Désordres de l'amour*, which he had himself published in 1675, by the popular Mme de Villedieu, and one of the stories composing which – the 'Histoire du Maréchal de Bellegarde' – contained, like *La Princesse de Clèves*, a contentious 'confession scene'. But there is evidence that Barbin had been granted a *privilège* (that is, an official monopoly) as far back as 1671 – i.e. four years before the publication of *Les Désordres de l'amour* – for a work (which never in fact appeared, but may have been the first germ of the text we have been studying) to be called *Le Prince de Clèves*.

To demonstrate the attribution of a work of literature beyond reasonable doubt is a legitimate and tempting scholarly aspiration. Clearly, knowledge of the identity of the author is part of the totality of truth. But, equally clearly, *Macbeth* would remain *Macbeth*, with all its possible layers of significance, were it to be shown conclusively that the play is not by Shakespeare. Even the discovery of irrefutable evidence of the intentions of its author – Shakespeare or another – would still leave us with most of those layers: the knowledge of what the author thought he was up to would help us to exclude no more than some of the wilder interpretations. As D.H. Lawrence once wrote: 'Never trust the artist, trust the tale'. Shortage of space in this little book dictates that fuller discussion of the question of the authorship of *La Princesse de Clèves* must be left to another occasion, and perhaps to other researchers. In the meantime, let us continue to admire the lucidity, literary skill, and prudence of the writer whom the nineteenth-century critic Sainte-Beuve[33] thought

Clèves', in *Hortulus amicorum. Fritz Ernst zum sechzigsten Geburtstag*, Zürich, 1949 (pp.11- 13).

[33] *Portraits de femmes*, Garnier, 1886, p.345, n. (in the essay on Mme de Longueville).

of as 'ma bonne, ma sage, ma judicieuse et sérieuse Mme de Lafayette', quietly observing, reflecting, and keeping her own counsel in the court circle of the Grande Mademoiselle and Lauzun.[34]

---

[34] *8*, IV, p.474.

Select Bibliography

Unless otherwise stated, the place of publication of items in English is London, those in French, Paris.

1. Le Breton, A., *Le Roman français au dix-septième siècle,* Hachette, 1890.
2. Magendie, M., *La Politesse mondaine et les théories de l'honnêteté, en France, au XVIIe siècle, de 1600 à 1660,* Alcan, 1925.
3. McDougall, Dorothy, *Madeleine de Scudéry: her romantic life and death,* Methuen, 1938.
4. Morrissette, B.A., *The Life and Works of Marie-Catherine Desjardins (Mme de Villedieu), 1632-1683* (Washington University Studies, New Series, Language & Literature No.17), Saint-Louis (Missouri), 1947.
5. Villedieu, Mme de, *Les Désordres de l'amour,* éd. Micheline Cuénin (Textes littéraires français, 174), Geneva, Droz, 1970.
5a. Lafayette, Mme de, *Histoire de la Princesse de Montpensier; Histoire de la Comtesse de Tende,* éd. Micheline Cuénin (Textes littéraires français, 267), Geneva, Droz, 1979. See also J.W. Scott, *Modern Language Review,* 50 (1955), pp.15-24. 'Criticism and *La Comtesse de Tende*'.
6. *Mémoires de Mme de Motteville sur Anne d'Autriche et sa cour,* éd. Riaux, 4 vols, Charpentier-Fasquelle, [1855].
7. Chamard, H., and Rudler, G., (a) 'Les sources historiques de *La Princesse de Clèves*'. *Revue du XVIe siècle,* II (1914), pp.92-131.

    (b) 'Les épisodes historiques de *La Princesse de Clèves*', *Revue du XVIe siècle,* II (1914), pp.290-321.

    (c) 'Les sources historiques de *La Princesse de Clèves*', *Revue du XVIe siècle,* V (1917-18), pp.1-20.

    (d) 'L'histoire et la fiction dans *La Princesse de Clèves*', *Revue du XVIe siècle,* V (1917-8), pp.231-43.
8. *Mémoires de Mlle de Montpensier,* éd. Chéruel, 4 vols, Charpentier, 1891.
9. Valincour, J.-B.-H. du Trousset de, *Lettres à Mme la Marquise*** sur le sujet de la Princesse de Clèves,* éd. A. Cazes, Bossard, 1926.
10. Pingaud, B., *Mme de Lafayette par elle-même,* Editions du Seuil, 1959.
11. Gregorio, L.A., *Order in the Court: history and society in 'La Princesse de Clèves'.* Stanford French & Italian Studies, 47, 1986.

12. *French Literature and its Background*, ed. J. Cruickshank, II, *The Seventeenth Century,* Oxford Paperbacks, 1969. Chapter 10 deals with prose fiction, and has appended to it brief biographical notes on some writers of the time, including Mme de Lafayette.

13. Malandain, P., *Madame de Lafayette, 'La Princesse de Clèves'*, P.U.F., 1985.

14. Campbell, J., *Questions of Interpretation in 'La Princesse de Clèves'*, Amsterdam/Atlanta. Rodopi, 1996. Contains a wide-ranging bibliography.

15. Green, Anne, *Privileged anonymity: the writings of Madame de Lafayette*, Oxford, Legenda (European Humanities Research Centre), 1996 (Research Monographs in French Studies, 1).

CRITICAL GUIDES TO FRENCH TEXTS

edited by
Roger Little, Wolfgang van Emden, David Williams